DEPARTMENT OF HEALTH AND SOCIAL SECURITY
WELSH OFFICE

Better Services for the Mentally Handicapped

Presented to Parliament by the Secretary of State
for Social Services and the Secretary of State for Wales
by Command of Her Majesty
June 1971

LONDON
HER MAJESTY'S STATIONERY OFFICE
Reprinted 1976

95p net

Cmnd. 4683

FOREWORD BY SECRETARY OF STATE FOR SOCIAL SERVICES AND SECRETARY OF STATE FOR WALES

Much of the groundwork for this Paper was done under the previous Government, who also launched in 1969 a new drive to improve hospital services for the mentally handicapped. We acknowledge the work which they initiated. But their plans to finance these improvements did not extend beyond 1971–72.

This Paper reflects the very substantial increases in expenditure on services for the mentally handicapped made possible by the Government's decision, referred to in paragraph 28 of the White Paper " New Policies for Public Spending " (Cmnd. 4515), to adjust forward expenditure plans to provide for an additional £110 million over the years 1971–72 to 1974–75 for the health and personal social services in Great Britain, particularly for the elderly and mentally handicapped, over and above the provision planned by the previous administration. It also describes the rate of progress thereafter which seems practicable on present assumptions about public expenditure in the longer term.

KEITH JOSEPH,
Secretary of State for Social Services.

PETER THOMAS,
Secretary of State for Wales.

CONTENTS

INTRODUCTION

1. There are probably about 120,000 people in England and Wales who are severely mentally handicapped, of whom about 50,000 are children. Many more are mildly mentally handicapped.

2. What does this mean? What special help is needed for these people and their families? What is done for them at present, and what ought to be done in future? Why has this Government, like the previous Government, given special priority to developing services for the mentally handicapped, and what does this entail?

3. This paper deals with these questions. Its main objects are:

(i) To explain why the present services need to be extended and improved, and the shift in emphasis from care in hospital to care in the community accelerated.

(ii) To invite greater sympathy and tolerance on the part of the public for the mentally handicapped in their own local communities, and to stress the importance of the help they can give through voluntary services.

(iii) To give local authorities and hospital authorities guidance on the lines on which the Government wish their services to develop.

(iv) To describe the programmes of improvement and development which have been started, and what more needs to be done.

4. The term "mental handicap" is used throughout this paper. Various other terms are used, here and in other countries, with the same meaning. "Mental deficiency" used to be the statutory term in England and Wales and still is in Scotland. In England and Wales the present statutory terms are "subnormality" and "severe subnormality", which together cover the conditions for which the term "mental handicap" is used in this paper. The term "mental retardation" is used in the United States and has also been adopted by the World Health Organisation with the sub-classifications "mild", "moderate", "severe" and "profound"; the last three of these together are broadly equivalent to the term "severe mental handicap" used in this paper. "Mental handicap" is used in preference to any of the alternative terms because this helps to emphasise that our attitude should be the same as to other types of handicap, i.e., to prevent it whenever possible, to assess it adequately when it occurs, and to do everything possible to alleviate its severity and compensate for its effects.

5. Description of our present services in Chapter 4 inevitably highlights their deficiencies. It needs to be made clear at the outset that this implies no criticism of the hospital or local authority staff who are concerned with the day-to-day care of the mentally handicapped in hospital or elsewhere. On the contrary, they, with the mentally handicapped themselves and their families, bear the brunt of these deficiencies.

6. The nurses, many working in overcrowded and understaffed hospital wards, are giving devoted personal service to their patients. We look to them with confidence to improve the quality of their patients' daily life when the means of doing so are put into their hands.

1

CHAPTER 1

MENTALLY HANDICAPPED PEOPLE AND THEIR FAMILIES

Mentally handicapped children and adults

What is mental handicap?

7. A person who is mentally handicapped does not develop in childhood as quickly as other children nor attain the full mental capacities of a normal adult. The handicap may be slight or severe. In the most severe cases, development does not progress even in adult life beyond the mental capacity of a young child; such severe handicap is much less common than milder degrees of handicap covering a wide spectrum ranging up to and merging into the "normal".

8. Mentally handicapped people have difficulty in understanding, and in adapting themselves to new situations. They may find it difficult to communicate, or to establish relationships with more than a few people, but they are generally affectionate and respond to affectionate treatment as children do. Many of those with severe mental handicap have physical handicaps as well, which are often also severe; they find it more difficult than other people to compensate for even a minor physical handicap. Some of the mentally handicapped also suffer from mental illness or personality disorders. But often mental handicap entails no more than slow and restricted development, uncomplicated by any other serious disability.

What are the causes?

9. In most cases the causes are not known. Mental handicap can result from conditions arising before or at birth which affect the functioning of the brain; some · of these are becoming rarer owing to improvement in the maternity services, but more children with very severe handicap are now surviving birth and infancy. It is often the result of unpredictable and unavoidable factors—hereditary or environmental or both—including the lower end of the normal range of variation of intelligence. In some cases the handicap is known to be due to an organic condition, such as a chromosome abnormality or metabolic disorder; in a few cases, some of these conditions can now be corrected if identified at an early stage.

Effects of other handicaps

10. Without very careful assessment, some children with disabilities of hearing, vision or language may be diagnosed as mentally handicapped because of their inability to communicate. Even when such a disability is clearly recognised, development may be delayed or in extreme cases permanently restricted, resulting in mental handicap, if the disability cannot be corrected or cured by special education or treatment. Some form of physical illness occurring in childhood may have a permanent effect on mental development and produce mental handicap.

2

11. A child's capacity to learn and develop may be restricted through social deprivation, particularly if the child or his parents are somewhat below average in intelligence; such children may improve remarkably if the emotional and intellectual stimulus of which they have been deprived can be provided.

Mental illness and mental handicap

12. Mental handicap is sometimes wrongly confused with mental illness. Mental illness can strike anyone at any age: it usually responds to treatment and can often be cured. Mental handicap, on the other hand, is usually determined before or during birth or in the early weeks of life and affects a person's ability to learn and reason. It cannot be "cured" in the same sense as an illness but the development of mentally handicapped people can often be improved by education, training and social care (and without such help may remain unnecessarily restricted). The physical and emotional disabilities which are often associated with mental handicap may be alleviated with special medical, nursing and educational treatment.

Prospects

13. Although the handicapped have a shorter expectation of life than the population as a whole, the majority live well into adult life and many into old age. There are many more mentally handicapped adults than children. The severely handicapped never become fully independent but need special help throughout their lives. Those with milder degrees of handicap need varying degrees and forms of support.

The effect on the family

14. Inevitably the presence of a severely handicapped child or adult causes great strain on the family as a whole. It may affect their whole way of life.

15. First there is the shock to the parents of learning that their child is handicapped. If there is also physical abnormality the handicap may be apparent at birth; otherwise it is usually recognised as the child fails to develop at the normal rate. The parents then know that they cannot look forward to the gradual lessening of their responsibilities which takes place as a normal child grows to maturity and independence.

16. Because a handicapped child may need for many years as much care and supervision as a very young normal child, it is often difficult for the parents to maintain an ordinary social life of their own. They may become isolated and lonely, which can increase the tensions of their family life and affect their own mental and physical health. If the child is physically as well as mentally handicapped, he becomes increasingly difficult to care for as he grows older; he can only be left at home if suitable care can be arranged and it becomes harder for the mother to take him out with her. Incontinence may be a serious problem.

17. Other children in the family may suffer if their parents' time and energy are exhausted by the physical and emotional demands of the handicapped child. Family holidays and recreation are difficult to arrange. The quality of home life for the whole family may be affected.

3

18.   Yet a handicapped child needs the affection and stimulating company which a family normally provides for its children.   Parents are often faced with acute problems in balancing the needs of a handicapped child with those of the rest of the family.

19.   As the child grows into an adult these problems do not necessarily diminish.   Indeed if the handicap is severe, they are likely to increase.   In addition, the parents become increasingly anxious about what will happen to their child when they cannot care for him any longer.

20.   Most parents are devoted to their handicapped children and wish to care for them and help them to develop to their full potential.   About 80 per cent of severely handicapped children and 40 per cent of severely handicapped adults—and a higher proportion of the more mildly handicapped—live at home.   Their families need advice and many forms of help, most of which at present are rarely available.

CHAPTER 2

NUMBERS

Surveys to provide information

21. We do not know precisely the prevalence of mental handicap nor the number of mentally handicapped people who require particular forms of help. Better information is needed, and is being obtained through surveys financed by the Department of Health and Social Security; some of their findings are already available.

Purpose of surveys

22. Paragraph 33 explains that precise estimates of prevalence are never likely to be obtained. For practical purposes these are not important. What we need is a reasonable basis for estimating the numbers of people for whom different types of services are likely to be required. Such estimates will provide planning targets, and their adequacy can be tested by experience of the calls made on the services as they develop. It is easier—and perhaps more important—to make such estimates in relation to people with severe mental handicap, than of those with milder handicap. The severely handicapped even when adult can rarely live independently; they and their families require special help not only while they are children but throughout their lives.

Information recorded by surveys

23. Three surveys have been carried out during the last few years, in the Wessex and Newcastle hospital regions and in the former metropolitan borough of Camberwell. They have recorded the number of people known to be receiving, on account of mental handicap, any form of health or personal social services from public authorities or in registered mental nursing homes or residential homes, and those known to need any such service but not to be receiving it. The numbers have been analysed by age, by the degree of mental handicap (measured by the intelligence quotient), by type and degree of certain physical and behaviour difficulties, and according to whether the handicapped people are living at home or elsewhere.

24. Table 1 summarises the result of the surveys in relation to people classified as having severe mental handicap, wherever resident; it also gives the numbers classified as having mild handicap who, when the surveys were made, were in hospital or other residential care. For the reasons explained below, the figures, even for severe handicap, should be interpreted as broad indications rather than precise findings.

25. The surveys also recorded other associated physical disabilities besides those mentioned in the Table. The Wessex survey found that among severely mentally handicapped children in hospital in that region 1 in 3 also suffered from epilepsy, 1 in 5 had defects of vision or hearing, and 1 in 20 were blind; among the severely mentally handicapped adults in hospital 1 in 5 suffered from epilepsy, 1 in 5 had defects of vision or hearing, and almost 1 in 3 had speech defects.

TABLE I

Incapacity Associated with Mental Handicap

(Taken from the surveys in Wessex, Newcastle and Camberwell)

Rate per 100,000 total population

Place of residence	Degree of mental handicap	Non-ambulant		Behaviour difficulties requiring constant supervision		Severely incontinent		Needing assistance to feed, wash or dress		No physical handicap or severe behaviour difficulties		Incapacity not assessed		Total	
		0–14 years	15+ years	0–14 years	15+ years	0–14 years	15+ years	0–14 years	15+ years	0–14 years	15+ years	0–14 years	15+ years	0–14 years	15+ years
Home ...	Severe	10·49	3·18	4·83	3·17	5·00	1·69	15·90	9·29	12·79	53·90	0·73	0·94	49·24	71·65
Hospital or other residential care	Severe	6·10	7·23	4·86	·15·58	3·65	6·97	3·63	16·58	1·69	49·36	0·10	0·94	19·96	96·19
	Mild	0·34	1·51	0·88	5·29	0·15	0·64	0·23	1·96	3·85	42·20	0·21	0·15	5·55	53·17
Total ...		16·81	11·92	10·27	24·01	8·75	9·30	19·68	27·82	17·04	146·46	1·04	3·03	72·90	221·00

These figures are averages of the findings of the three surveys mentioned in paragraph 23.

Severe mental handicap

26. An intelligence quotient of 50 is commonly taken as a broad dividing line between mild and severe handicap (though such a division is of little practical importance to people near either side of it). The intelligence quotient as measured by tests of various kinds is not a precise measure of a person's ability, and can change quite substantially during life. Mental handicap is not to be measured in terms of intelligence alone; emotional development is also relevant. Nevertheless, the intelligence quotient has less subjective errors than other criteria, and is a useful indicator. The three surveys used IQ 50 either as their sole criterion or as one of their criteria in distinguishing the two categories of mild or severe handicap.

27. It is generally believed that by the end of adolescence nearly all people with severe mental handicap are known to the hospital or local authorities, because they will have been identified during school age if not earlier or in the early years of employment. The survey findings for severe mental handicap in the 15–19 age group are therefore likely to be close to the true total. The findings of these three surveys are in broad agreement with others conducted elsewhere in Great Britain and Northern Ireland in indicating a prevalence of about 4 severely mentally handicapped per 1,000 population in this age group.

28. As severe mental handicap is generally present at birth, the prevalence rate in children must be at least as high as in adolescents. The surveys recorded lower rates. This indicates that many young children with such handicap are not known to the public services.

29. As age increases, the proportion of the population with severe mental handicap falls because they do not live as long as the population as a whole. This is the reason why it is estimated that total present numbers with severe mental handicap are probably about 120,000 (between 2 and 3 per 1,000 population, compared with 4 per 1,000 at age 15–19). There is however evidence that the rate of survival is increasing.

Mild mental handicap

30. Mild mental handicap covers a wide range from the borderline with severe handicap to the borderline with people whose intelligence is below normal but to whom this does not present a significant handicap. There is no measurable dividing line at the upper end of the range.

31. Many people who have an intelligence quotient above about 50 but below the normal range are not materially affected by this and can lead ordinary lives. Others in this IQ range are unable to cope with the problems of living in society; they may then be regarded as mildly mentally handicapped and eligible for help from the local authority or hospital mental health services. These include some young people who may have been classified as educationally subnormal while at school. In adolescence such people may have difficulty in finding and keeping employment and adjusting to the requirements of adult life; at that stage they may need help from the mental health services but later manage without further support.

7

32. The number of such people who need such help is also related to the social conditions in which they live, educational services and opportunities for employment. Moreover the number seeking help, and therefore known to the authorities and through them to the surveys, depends partly on the services available locally, and these vary widely from one area to another.

33. For all these reasons we are never likely to obtain precise estimates of prevalence of mild mental handicap. It is difficult even to estimate the numbers requiring services except through experience of the use made of services actually provided. As the services are still at an early stage of development in most areas, such experience is not yet available.

34. Table 1 includes information from the surveys about the mildly mentally handicapped who are in hospital or other residential care, but does not give figures for those living at home. The reason for this is that those in hospital or other residential care are all known to the authorities, and the numbers are likely to be near the total of those requiring residential care of one sort or another. Those living at home are not all known to the authorities, for the reasons mentioned in paragraphs 30 to 33; the numbers recorded in the surveys varied widely and do not form a useful basis for estimating service needs.

National censuses of the mentally handicapped in hospital and in other residential accommodation

35. In order to obtain detailed information about mentally handicapped people now in hospital and in residential homes in the community, the Department of Health and Social Security and Welsh Office arranged for two censuses in 1970.

36. The first census was carried out by local authorities on 30 April 1970 and the information was sent to the central Departments for analysis. It covered all mentally handicapped people in local authority and voluntary homes in England and Wales. The information collected included the number of residents and the character of their mental and physical handicaps and degree of social dependence. This census is to be extended this year, in a modified form, to private homes for the mentally handicapped.

37. The second was a census of all mentally handicapped patients in hospitals in England and Wales on 31 December 1970. It covered not only patients in hospitals for the mentally handicapped but also mentally handicapped patients in other hospitals in the National Health Service and in hospitals or nursing homes outside the National Health Service who are being cared for under contract with a Regional Hospital Board. It recorded, among other information, the number of such patients and the character of their handicaps. Similar information is being collected about all mentally handicapped patients admitted from 1 January 1971 onwards.

38. The information from these two censuses is now being analysed. It will provide a further check on the findings of the surveys on questions which were covered both by the surveys and by the censuses, and new information on other questions. This should be of considerable value in planning services for the future.

CHAPTER 3

GENERAL PRINCIPLES

39. Chapter 4 describes the state of our present services for mental handicap. Chapters 5 and 6 discuss in detail present views on the services required and how they should be organised. Chapter 7 discusses the important role of voluntary services. The main principles on which current thinking about mental handicap is based need first to be stated.

40. These can be summarised as follows:

(i) A family with a handicapped member has the same needs for general social services as all other families. The family and the handicapped child or adult also need special additional help, which varies according to the severity of the handicap, whether there are associated physical handicaps or behaviour problems, the age of the handicapped person and his family situation.

(ii) Mentally handicapped children and adults should not be segregated unnecessarily from other people of similar age, nor from the general life of the local community.

(iii) Full use should be made of available knowledge which can help to prevent mental handicap or to reduce the severity of its effects.

(iv) There should be a comprehensive initial assessment and periodic reassessment of the needs of each handicapped person and his family.

(v) Each handicapped person needs stimulation, social training and education and purposeful occupation or employment in order to develop to his maximum capacity and to exercise all the skills he acquires, however limited they may be.

(vi) Each handicapped person should live with his own family as long as this does not impose an undue burden on them or him, and he and his family should receive full advice and support. If he has to leave home for a foster home, residential home or hospital, temporarily or permanently, links with his own family should normally be maintained.

(vii) The range of services in every area should be such that the family can be sure that their handicapped member will be properly cared for when it becomes necessary for him to leave the family home.

(viii) When a handicapped person has to leave his family home, temporarily or permanently, the substitute home should be as homelike as possible, even if it is also a hospital. It should provide sympathetic and constant human relationships.

(ix) There should be proper co-ordination in the application of relevant professional skills for the benefit of individual handicapped people and their families, and in the planning and administration of relevant services, whether or not these cross administrative frontiers.

(x) Local authority personal social services for the mentally handicapped should develop as an integral part of the services recently brought together under the Local Authority Social Services Act, 1970.

9

(xi) There should be close collaboration between these services and those provided by other local authority departments (*e.g.* child health services and education), and with general practitioners, hospitals and other services for the disabled.

(xii) Hospital services for the mentally handicapped should be easily accessible to the population they serve. They should be associated with other hospital services, so that a full range of specialist skills is easily available when needed for assessment or treatment.

(xiii) Hospital and local authority services should be planned and operated in partnership; the Government's proposals for the reorganisation of the National Health Service will encourage the closest co-operation.

(xiv) Voluntary service can make a contribution to the welfare of mentally handicapped people and their families at all stages of their lives and wherever they are living.

(xv) Understanding and help from friends and neighbours and from the community at large are needed to help the family to maintain a normal social life and to give the handicapped member as nearly normal a life as his handicap or handicaps permit.

CHAPTER 4

THE SERVICES TODAY

Historical background

41. Although the first Mental Deficiency Act was passed in 1913, its implementation on any scale was delayed by the war of 1914–18. The foundations of our present services were laid in the 1920s and 1930s. Attitudes to the mentally handicapped, views on services needed and the statutory responsibilities of public authorities were then very different from those underlying the principles which are now generally accepted and are summarised in Chapter 3.

Segregation of the mentally handicapped

42. Although there have always been more mentally handicapped people living with their families than anywhere else, it was thought best in those days that those who could not be cared for at home should be segregated from the rest of society in institutions—or " colonies " as they were often called. Even among those who lived at home many of the severely handicapped were hidden away by their families, and few mixed socially with their neighbours.

43. Most of the institutions or colonies were in the country, some distance from the towns, and were run as self-sufficient enclosed communities. Most of their inmates, once admitted, remained for life. This was considered to be in their best interests, to provide a sheltered environment in which comprehensive care was available for the mildly as well as the seriously handicapped, segregated from the rest of society. Less was known then than now about the extent to which the mentally handicapped may respond to the stimulus of education, training and social activity.

Responsibilities of local authorities before 1948

44. Until 1948, local authorities (counties and county boroughs) were responsible for all aspects of the care of the mentally handicapped. They had a duty to provide " supervision " and training or occupation for those not living in institutions, and institutions for those who could not be cared for at home.

Institutions for social as well as medical need

45. The inmates of the institutions included not only those with severe mental handicap, but also people with mild handicap who were " without visible means of support or cruelly treated ", or " in need of care and training which could not be provided in his home" or requiring "supervision" after leaving school. Many of these helped run the institutions as domestics, laundry workers, kitchen helps and gardeners. Their work contributed significantly to the care of the severely handicapped.

46. The institutions thus served a social welfare as well as a medical purpose. The Superintendent was usually a doctor, and most of the staff caring for the inmates were " attendants " and later nurses (helped by other inmates).

11

Changes in 1948

47. When the National Health Service started in 1948 these institutions were transferred to the new hospital authorities. At that time the accommodation in the former public assistance institutions, which had also previously performed both social welfare and medical functions, was divided between the new hospital authorities and the local authorities who remained responsible for providing residential accommodation for the elderly. But there was no similar apportionment of accommodation in the mental deficiency institutions, which all became " hospitals ". Local authorities continued to have a duty to provide services for the mentally handicapped living at home, but ceased to provide residential accommodation. The hospitals continued to admit the mentally handicapped who needed residential care on either social or medical grounds.

48. Within the hospital and local authority service the mentally handicapped continued, generally speaking, to be segregated. For example, while the local authorities' new children's departments might receive mentally handicapped children into care if the relevant criteria were satisfied (drawing on health and education services as a parent would), it was usual for all care for severely mentally handicapped children outside hospital to be provided by the mental health department; if residential care was needed the child was put on the waiting list for admission to hospital. The hospitals continued, in most areas, to have few links with other parts of the new hospital service, and most of them had their own separate Hospital Management Committees.

The Royal Commission of 1954–57

Emphasis on community care and end of segregation

49. These arrangements were reviewed by the Royal Commission which reported in 1957.* It recommended radical changes with a new emphasis on community care and breaking down segregation.

50. The Commission's general approach was very similar to present thinking as reflected in the principles summarised in Chapter 3. It recommended that all the general social services should be available to the mentally handicapped as well as others and that mental health services should be fully integrated with other health and welfare services. Hospitals should be responsible only for those requiring specialist medical treatment or training or continual nursing supervision; out-patient services should be provided. Local authorities should provide small residential homes or hostels for adults and children who cannot remain at home but do not need to be in hospital; these should not be isolated but in centres of population, and the residents should take part in the life of the local community. More training centres should be provided for children and adults in the community, more sheltered workshops and more social support for the mentally handicapped and their families.

Changes in 1959

51. These recommendations were accepted by the Government of the day and commended to local authorities and hospitals in circulars issued in 1959 and 1960. Those which required legislation were included in the

---

* Report of the Royal Commission on the Law relating to Mental Illness and Mental Deficiency, 1954–57; Cmnd. 169.

Mental Health Act 1959. In August 1959 the Minister of Health, by a direction under the National Health Service Act 1946 and the new Act, laid a duty on the local authorities to provide a full range of community services for the mentally handicapped, including residential accommodation. This replaced their previous duties under the Mental Deficiency Acts to provide " supervision ", training and occupation for those not in hospital.

New work for local authorities

52. Thus some 10 years after they had lost this function, and with it the accommodation they had formerly provided for the purpose, local authorities once more became responsible for residential care for the mentally handicapped. They were faced with the task not only of building up residential homes from scratch, but also of greatly expanding day services which they had formerly provided only on a relatively small scale.

Priorities

53. A choice had to be made in the use of resources. Most authorities, rightly, gave first priority in the field of mental handicap to training facilities; in this they have made excellent progress. More recently and in their present forward planning more attention has been given to residential homes.

54. Residential accommodation is still far short of what is needed to absorb the yearly flow of mentally handicapped people needing residential care outside their own homes but not the full medical and nursing service of a hospital. For lack of enough local authority homes therefore, and lack of other services which might make it possible for their own families to continue to care for them, such people are still pressing upon overcrowded hospital waiting lists.

Local authority services now

55. The strengths and weaknesses of the present community services stem from this historical background, and from the priorities adopted by different local authorities in the face of financial constraints. Generally speaking, the quality of the new training centres and residential homes provided in the last decade is good, because they are new and conform to modern standards. But, apart from junior training centres (now special schools) for children to which most authorities gave first priority, only a small start has been made towards providing in sufficient quantity training centres for mentally handicapped adults, residential care for adults and children, and practical help and advice for families with mentally handicapped members living at home.

Good new buildings

56. Most of the money spent by local authorities on the mentally handicapped in the past 10 years has been used for new training centres or residential homes in purpose-built or well-adapted buildings; these provide an excellent environment for services of a high standard. They do not have the problems of isolation from which the hospitals suffer; these local authority services are in the area where they are needed, easily accessible. Overcrowding is not a serious problem; in recent purpose-built residential

homes for mentally handicapped adults the majority of the residents have single rooms, and the homes are well furnished. Running costs are relatively high but reflect a service fully acceptable by modern standards.

Schools for children

57. Until 1 April 1971, when local education authorities became responsible for the education of mentally handicapped children, the more severely handicapped were excluded from the educational system. The training of those living at home was the responsibility of the local authorities' health departments; hospital authorities were responsible for those in hospital. The change in responsibility is the natural consequence of the considerable advances already made by health and hospital authorities in meeting the educational needs of mentally handicapped children.

Numbers

58. In the 1960s, local authorities gave first priority to increasing the number of junior training centres for mentally handicapped children living at home, to replacing unsatisfactory old buildings and to separating the training of children from that of adults. The number of places rose from 12,200 in 1960 to 23,500 at the end of 1970. The number of centres rose to over 700, of which less than 100 provided for adults in the same buildings, compared with 458 centres in 1960 of which 266 also provided for adults.

Variations between authorities

59. But there are still wide variations between authorities, and some local shortages. Some authorities have set their sights high and have already reached their targets. But in other areas there are children unable to attend for lack of places, or because their homes are too far away for them to attend unless boarding facilities are provided. At the end of 1969 about 1,800 children were on waiting lists for places in junior training centres.

60. After taking into account the use made of centres run by other local authorities or voluntary organisations, the number of places provided at the end of 1969 per 1,000 population aged 5–14 varied from less than 2 (by 2 authorities) to over 7 (by 4 authorities) with a mean of 3·16. These variations may be connected to some extent with where in the past different authorities drew the line between special schools for children classified as educationally subnormal and their junior training centres.

General quality

61. Nevertheless, the health departments have handed over to the education departments a service which, overall, has improved out of all recognition in the last decade.

Special care units

62. Most local health authorities provided " special care units ", usually as part of a junior training centre, for mentally handicapped children who also had such severe physical handicaps or behaviour disorders that they could not attend a normal class in the centre. This helps parents to keep at home children who would otherwise need to be admitted to hospital. At the end of 1969 there were 187 such units attached to junior training centres, providing places for about 2,500 children, and 28 separate units with 780

14

places. These have now been transferred to the local education authorities. For adults who are unable to benefit from the usual adult training centre programme there are special facilities in a few areas in the form of units for "adult special care" or "pre-vocational training".

63. There has been some argument whether, especially for adults, "special care" should be regarded as a function for the local authorities or whether this sort of care should be provided, on a day basis, by hospitals. Certainly most (but not all) of these children and adults require some specialist medical and nursing attention, together with special services such as speech therapy or physiotherapy to deal with particular disabilities; the children also need education and the adults further education and training. There is therefore scope for the development both of special care units by local authorities and of day places in hospitals. In many cases it will be desirable for hospitals and local authorities to arrange joint provision of appropriate staff and contributions to the running costs.

Training and occupation for adults

64. Adult training centres provide further training, and in many cases permanent daily occupation, for mentally handicapped adults who are not able to work in open or sheltered employment. Although progress has been made in improving and increasing these, many more places are still needed.

Not enough

65. The number of places for adults rose from 10,100 in 1960 to 26,400 by the end of 1970, but there are many areas where the increase is still barely sufficient to take in the young people who leave the junior training centres (now special schools) each year. Older adolescents have to remain in the school or at home until a place in an adult centre can be found. Many older adults remain at home without training or daily occupation and with little prospect of the opportunity of a place in a training centre. A survey of 26 adult training centres undertaken in 1969 showed that 37 per cent of those attending were aged 16–20; 39 per cent were aged 21–30; less than a quarter were over 30.

66. There are wide variations between different local authorities. After taking into account the use made of centres run by other local authorities or voluntary organisations, the number of places provided at the end of 1969 per 1,000 population aged 15–64 varied from 0·4 or less (by 7 authorities) to over 2·0 (by 6 authorities) with a mean of only 0·78 places. This is quite insufficient even for the adults now living at home or in residential care outside hospital; for this purpose about 1·5 places per 1,000 population aged 15–64 are needed—nearly twice the present number. The requirement increases as the number of mentally handicapped adults living in residential care outside hospital increases. For the long-term future, when in addition to all these it may also be desirable for these centres to provide places for substantial numbers of adults coming by day from the hospitals (as discussed in Chapter 5), a target of 2·4 places per 1,000 population in this age group is suggested. No authority has yet reached this target and the great majority are very far indeed from even the interim target of 1·5 places.

Residential care

67. As mentioned in paragraphs 51 and 52, in 1959 local authorities were again put under a duty to provide residential accommodation for the mentally handicapped, but had to start building this up again from scratch. They have begun to implement this duty by building (or adapting) residential homes which they run themselves and by placing mentally handicapped people in homes run by other local authorities or by voluntary organisations or private individuals or in private households or supervised lodgings.

Gross shortage

68. At the end of 1969, 24 of the 157 local authorities in England and 4 of the 17 authorities in Wales still had no arrangements of this sort at all either for children or adults. Another 64 in England and 5 in Wales had no such arrangements for children, and 28 in England and 3 in Wales no arrangements for adults. 37 authorities in England and 1 in Wales had no residential homes of their own but had arranged some placements elsewhere. 13 in England and 2 in Wales had one or more homes of their own for children, but none for adults. 44 in England and 6 in Wales had one or more homes of their own for adults but none for children. Only 39 English authorities and 4 Welsh had provided homes of their own for both children and adults.

Children

69. The total number of places in homes for children in England and Wales at the end of 1969, including use of places in voluntary or private homes, was about 1,800. 1,300 of these were in the 68 residential homes run by the authorities themselves, many of which were used as boarding homes, five days a week, by children attending junior training centres but living too far away to travel daily. In addition about 70 children were placed with private families or foster homes. The total of 1,870 children in residential care arranged by local authorities represents 0·16 per 1,000 population aged 0–14. Chapter 5 suggests that such residential care is needed for 0·52 per 1,000 in this age group.

Adults

70. For adults, there were about 4,350 places in residential homes at the end of 1969, and 550 placed in private households or lodgings, a total of 4,900 in residential care arranged by local authorities. About 3,200 of these were in 151 residential homes run by the authorities themselves. In addition about 1,700 mentally handicapped adults under age 65 were unsuitably living in homes for the elderly provided under the National Assistance Act, including former public assistance institutions. The total of 4,900 adults in suitable residential care represents 0·13 per 1,000 population aged 15 or over. Chapter 5 suggests that such care is needed for 0·98 per 1,000 adults.

Present building plans

71. Since the end of 1969, 106 new places for children and 287 new places for adults have been provided in local authority homes, and 183 places for children and 687 for adults are under construction. But even if local authorities' plans for the next 3 years to March 1974 can be carried out in

16

full, 59 authorities in England and 8 in Wales will then still have no homes of their own for mentally handicapped children and 14 authorities in England and 1 in Wales none for adults.

Effect of shortage

72. As the figures show, in many parts˙ of the country facilities for residential care outside hospital are still nil or minimal.

73. Lack of experience in providing residential services can result in places in the few residential homes that exist being used for people who could manage with a lesser degree of support in suitable lodgings. Places in some homes may remain empty because they are reserved for a special purpose for which the demand is limited, or which is wrongly thought to have priority over other needs.

74. The main effect of shortage of residential places, combined with shortage in many areas of training centres and of social workers, is that some families with mentally handicapped members living at home have to continue under almost unbearable stress and many hospitals are under unrelenting pressure to admit more patients to already overcrowded wards.

Shortage of trained staff

75. Shortage of staff, particularly trained staff, is a limiting factor on the quality and further development of every part of the local authority services. There is a shortage of social workers who are needed to support families and the mentally handicapped themselves, and staff for training centres and residential homes.

Social workers

76. The number of trained social workers is increasing, but there are still not nearly enough to give every family with a mentally handicapped member the support it should have. The amalgamation of social services into one department of each local authority should help to provide a better standard of care for families of the mentally handicapped by bringing together teams consisting of social workers with a variety of special skills and knowledge. For example, social workers trained in child care will be available in these departments to add their contribution to the care of mentally handicapped children. In 1969 about 2,000 mental health social workers were employed by local authorities, of whom just over 600˙ had had training in social work. More qualifying and in-service training is planned, including training directed specially toward the social problems resulting from mental handicap.

Staff of adult training centres

77. The total number of staff in adult training centres is adequate for the present number of trainees, but nearly three-quarters of the staff are still unqualified. Until courses were started under the auspices of the Training Council for Teachers of the Mentally Handicapped, which was set up in 1964, there was no specific training for this work apart from one pioneer course run by the National Association for Mental Health. There

are now courses, mainly in Colleges of Further Education, from which about 170 people a year qualify for the Training Council's Diploma; about two-thirds of these in recent years have been training centre staff seconded by local authorities.

78. The proportion of qualified staff is therefore increasing, but while so many of those employed are still unqualified there is a danger of imbalance in the work of the training centres—for example too much emphasis on production and contract work at the expense of a progressive programme of social and work training, recreation and further education.

Staff of residential homes

79. Even for the small number of residential homes which exist now, it is difficult to find staff, especially trained staff. Existing staff are people with various forms of previous experience. Some have been trained for their previous work, but not for this work. Without appropriate training, they may be inclined to over-protection of the residents, thus limiting their progress towards greater self-reliance and independence. Special training has only recently started, and will fall to be developed by the new Central Council for Education and Training in Social Work.

Summary of local authority services

80. It is right to acknowledge the progress made by the local authorities in the last 10 years in developing good quality services for the mentally handicapped in the community. But in national terms these are still grossly deficient in quantity. In particular there is a serious shortage of adult training centres, gross shortage of residential accommodation, and great need for more trained staff of all kinds. The developments recommended by the Royal Commission 14 years ago are far from being accomplished. The Government's plans for faster progress are described in Chapter 6.

Hospital services now

81. The difficulties which hospitals for the mentally handicapped are now facing stem partly from the inheritance of history—isolation, old and unsuitable buildings, large numbers of patients who need a protective environment but not hospital care. They are also due to changes during the last two decades in the make-up of their patient-population, and changes in public and professional attitudes towards the mentally handicapped. Most of the hospitals have not had the resources with which some of their difficulties could be overcome, and some of the difficulties are insuperable without changes in the location of hospitals and substantial development of local authority services.

Changes in patient population

82. The total number of patients in hospitals used wholly for the mentally handicapped, or in units set aside for the mentally handicapped in other hospitals, has changed little in the last 15 years. It has varied between 54,000 and 60,000. Within this total there have been two substantial and significant changes. There is now a much higher proportion of severely handicapped patients, and a very different age distribution.

More severely handicapped

83. Precise figures of the proportion of severely and mildly handicapped patients are not available for past years, to compare with the figures now being obtained from the surveys and censuses mentioned in Chapter 2. But it is common knowledge that patients admitted in recent years include a higher proportion suffering from severe mental and physical handicap, and that they are surviving longer than in the past. At the same time, the number of mildly handicapped who used to assist in the running of the hospitals has dropped. This is probably due partly to the development of community services, particularly training centres, which has made it easier for those with mild handicap to remain with their families, and partly to the success of the hospitals in rehabilitating and discharging more of the less handicapped patients.

More older patients

84. The change in age distribution is clear from Table 2.

TABLE 2

Patients resident in National Health Service hospitals, or hospital units, for the mentally handicapped

	Age 0–14	15–54	55 and over	Total
1954	7,000*	45,700*	5,500*	58,100*
1963	6,900	40,300	11,200	58,400
1968	6,600	39,300	13,500	59,400
1969	6,400	38,600	13,850	58,850

*The 1954 figures include some 4,000 patients living in the community "on licence" after discharge who cannot be allocated to age-groups; most are likely to have been in the 15–54 age-group.

85. The fall in the number of children since 1963 may reflect the development of local authority services for children outside hospital. There has been a small but steady fall in the 15–54 age group, and a striking increase in the number of older patients.

Effect of these changes

86. The increased proportion of severely handicapped patients combined with the increased proportion of elderly patients has produced a patient population which makes greater demands on the nursing staff and contains fewer who are able to help in domestic and other jobs within the hospital.

Change in attitudes

87. The old custodial attitudes have gradually been replaced by the more positive attitudes underlying the principles summarised in Chapter 3. This is partly the result of work done in the hospitals and elsewhere which has demonstrated that even the severely handicapped have previously unrecognised capabilities for development of manual and other skills and varying degrees of social independence if they receive the necessary stimulus and appropriate education and other forms of training.

88. Other contributing factors have been greater public awareness of, and sympathy towards, the mentally handicapped and their families; more open discussion of the subject; and general expectation that the mentally

19

handicapped should receive services of as high a quality as the state provides for any other group of disabled children or adults. The National Society for Mentally Handicapped Children, the National Association for Mental Health and other voluntary bodies, and their local associations, have played a large part in bringing about this change in public attitudes.

New demands

89. In the hospitals this has meant demands for more space, more equipment and more staff for teaching, play and recreation, occupational and industrial therapy. Higher standards of clothing, furnishing and decor are expected, in line with the changing standards and fashions of the times. Physiotherapy, speech therapy and other special services are recognised as necessary for the proper treatment of disabled patients. More individual attention to the social, medical and nursing needs of individual patients is known to be needed. Contact with the world outside the hospital, and with patients' families, is known to be beneficial.

90. Almost all hospitals have introduced some improvements to meet some of these new demands. But very few have had the resources to do anything like as much as the staff themselves want to do. On the contrary, the increasing pressures of having to deal with more heavily handicapped patients in unsuitable buildings with too few staff have only too often led to falling rather than rising standards, as described in more detail in the rest of this Chapter.

Isolation and size

91. When many of the present hospitals were built, or when country houses were acquired to be adapted and extended for use as "institutions" for the mentally handicapped, isolation from the surrounding community and substantial size were considered advantages. Now isolation and size present serious problems.

Difficult to get to

92. A large hospital necessarily serves a large population. Contact between hospital staff and patients' families, general practitioners and local health authorities is very difficult; so is visiting by relatives. Consultants from the hospital cannot easily hold out-patient clinics throughout the area served. Day patients cannot get to the hospital. It is difficult to recruit enough domestic and other staff locally.

Isolation of staff

93. If the hospital is isolated, whatever its size, the same difficulties arise or are exacerbated. Isolation also affects professional work, cutting off staff and patients from the rest of medicine, nursing and social work, and tending to inhibit the dissemination and application of ideas and methods, including methods of management, which have proved beneficial in other hospitals.

Size

94. At the end of 1969 7 of our hospitals for the mentally handicapped contained over 1,500 beds; 2 of these had over 2,000. Another 3 clusters of hospitals administered as single hospitals had over 1,500. 33 hospitals

or clusters of hospitals had between 500 and 1,500 beds. Since the early 1960s the policy has been not to plan any new hospital for the mentally handicapped for more than 500 patients, but some new larger hospitals whose planning started earlier have recently come into use. Some of these are remote as well, and have wards empty because staff cannot be recruited.

95. There are also many smaller hospitals. In 1969 there were over 50 with between 100 and 500 beds and nearly 50 with less than 100 beds. But many of these are associated with larger hospitals and with them take patients from all parts of a single catchment area. Small hospitals therefore at present are sometimes just as remote from the population they serve as the larger ones.

Unsuitable buildings

96. About £30 million has been spent since 1948 by Regional Hospital Boards on new hospitals for the mentally handicapped and on large schemes of adaptation, improvement or extension. Nevertheless many of the hospital buildings still in use are very old and originally built for other purposes; half of today's patients are in hospitals over sixty years old. Even hospitals built in the 1920s and 1930s do not have sanitation or heating acceptable on present standards unless they have had substantial adaptations.

97. Even more important is that most of the present hospital buildings were designed for custodial care, and for less severely handicapped patients. It is extremely hard, though creditable attempts have been made, to create a homely atmosphere in a barrack-like institutional building; or to care for severely handicapped incontinent patients in multi-storey buildings without lifts, or with lavatories on one floor and the rooms used during the day on another.

98. Few hospitals built over ten years ago originally included the space now considered necessary for education, industrial and occupational therapy and leisure activities. Additions have been made to many hospitals, and dormitories converted, for this purpose. But all too often this is still not enough. Activities such as industrial therapy often take place in many different parts of a large hospital site, which can make the organisation of a progressive therapeutic programme difficult if not impossible.

Overcrowding

99. Almost all the hospitals are overcrowded, or have some overcrowded wards. A survey in 1969 showed that less than 10 per cent of all patients had the 70 sq. ft. per patient in bedrooms and dormitories and 48 sq. ft. per patient in dining and living rooms which are recommended as the desirable minimum. Nearly 60 per cent had less than 50 sq. ft. sleeping space and over 40 per cent had less than 30 sq. ft. in day rooms.

Little activity or privacy

100. In many hospitals the most overcrowded wards are those containing severely handicapped patients, many of them incontinent, who remain in the wards all day for lack of facilities for occupation elsewhere in the hospital. In such wards there is not enough room—even if there were enough staff— to give the patients any stimulating occupation. At night they sleep in dormitories with scarcely enough room to move between serried ranks of

beds. There is no room to keep stocks of personal clothes, and no space for cupboards or lockers for patients' other possessions. As a result they are not given clothes of their own or other possessions, even if this is done in other parts of the hospital.

Little treatment

101. In such conditions hospital " treatment " is restricted to meeting the patients' most basic physical needs. The nurses' time is taken up in getting patients up in the morning, dressing, washing and feeding them, dealing with incontinence during the day and putting them to bed in the evening. It is a life of minimal satisfaction for patients and staff alike.

Efforts to introduce activity

102. These are the extreme results of overcrowding combined with under-staffing. There are all gradations between this and real success in introducing activity and a sense of purpose into even seriously overcrowded wards.

Reasons for overcrowding

103. It is difficult for a hospital, however full it may be, to refuse to admit a severely handicapped person whose presence at home is putting unbearable strain on his family. It is difficult to turn away a person with any degree of handicap who is not capable of fending for himself and becomes homeless through the death of relatives or through their moving to a house without room for him, if there are no alternative facilities for residential care outside hospital. These are the circumstances in which many hospitals have continued to tolerate gross overcrowding.

Joint remedies

104. Overcrowding has been a severe problem for these hospitals for many years. All Regional Hospital Boards have made improvements and extensions in an attempt to overcome it, or at least keep pace with the pressure to admit more patients. In the last 18 months a more vigorous attack on the problem has been launched, as described in Chapter 6. But the solution does not lie only in the hands of the hospital authorities. It also lies with the local authorities, through the improvement of domiciliary and other services to make it reasonably possible for families to keep mentally handicapped children and adults in their homes, and through the provision of residential care for those who need it but do not need to be in hospital.

Living standards

105. As well as being overcrowded buildings are often dilapidated and poorly furnished. In many hospitals there has not been enough money, or not enough imagination, to buy modern furniture, to repaint wards in bright colours, to provide each patient with clothes of his own in modern styles, or even to provide good and varied food. In many there is not enough space to give every patient a cupboard of his own for his own clothes and personal possessions.

106. In other hospitals these things have been done, and patients have appreciated them. Some hospitals provide good quality clothes for each individual patient. Some provide excellent food. In some, all patients have a cupboard or locker for their personal possessions. Some have good

22

modern furniture, gay curtains and carpets and bedspreads.   Toys and playthings are excellent in some hospitals.   But few if any have had enough money to afford all these things for all their patients.   In the last 18 months all Hospital Boards have been given targets of improvements to achieve minimum standards of amenity, and money with which to start doing so.

Staffing

Causes of under-staffing

107.   Isolation and insufficient money have together contributed to serious under-staffing in many hospitals.   Shortage of finance has limited the total numbers employed; the size and location of many hospitals has made it difficult to find sufficient staff locally; and poor working conditions have made it hard to attract new recruits.

Nurses, domestic staff and doctors

108.   The number of nurses (including student and pupil nurses and nursing assistants) in hospitals used solely for the mentally handicapped rose, in whole-time equivalents, from 10,000 in 1959 to 14,600 in 1969; including units for the mentally handicapped in other hospitals, the number in 1969 was 15,200.   Domestic staff rose from 1,900 whole-time equivalents in 1965 to 2,700 in 1969.   But these numbers are still insufficient to allow nurses to care properly for heavily handicapped patients, to give all patients the personal interest and social stimulation they require, and to relieve the nurses of domestic work.

109.   The number of medical, nursing and domestic staff in 1969 are given in Table 3, which also shows the range of variation between different hospitals.   Some of the variations are accounted for by differences in the proportion of children and of severely handicapped patients, by whether other specialist staff or nurses provide their education, training and occupation, and by the amount of domestic work done by patients or domestic staff.

TABLE 3

Staff of hospitals and hospital units for the mentally handicapped, September 1969

	Number in whole-time equivalents	Average ratio of staff to patients	Range of ratios of staff to patients in hospitals of 300 or more beds	
			Highest	Lowest
All medical staff*	321	1 : 192	1 : 72	1 : 400
Nurses— Qualified ... ... Other	8,754 6,475	} 1 : 3·86	1 : 2	1 : 6·2
Domestic staff (including ward orderlies but excluding kitchen staff and porters) ...	2,725	1 : 22	1 : 7·35	1 : 500

* Excluding specialists without regular sessions who may be called on to treat or examine patients when occasion arises *e.g.*, surgeons, neurologists, paediatricians, etc.

23

110. Nursing is a 24-hour service; all nurses are not on duty together. A study in 1965–66 showed that there was then on average one member of the nursing staff on duty in the ward during the day to nearly 16 adults and 1 to 11 children. The ratio varied in different hospitals between 1 : 10 and 1 : 34 adults and between 1 : 6 and 1 : 16 children. In most large hospitals there is often only one enrolled nurse on duty in each ward at night; some wards share one nurse between them.

Other staff shortages

111. In general, the standard of staffing is such that in many hospitals it is not possible to give the individual attention which the staff know is needed and wish to give. Many of the skills needed for assessment, education, training and treatment are not provided.

Effect of shortages

112. Doctors responsible for several hundred in-patients cannot easily hold many out-patient clinics. Nor can they regularly reassess the progress of each in-patient and plan individual treatment and training. Nor can such a plan be implemented where medical and other staff are not available to carry it out.

113. Opportunities for modifying disturbed behaviour and incontinence by individual attention cannot be taken.

114. In the worst places this produces boredom and tension and even occasional violence. Patients become apathetic and institutionalised, and sink into a state of complete physical and social dependence. Nurses are frustrated by having no time to provide more than attention to basic physical needs, without using the psychiatric nursing skills in which they have been trained. They often have to clean the wards themselves for lack of domestic staff.

Management

115. In 1970 the new National Health Service Hospital Advisory Service sent teams of professional officers to visit all hospitals for the mentally handicapped in more than half of the English hospital regions and in the whole of Wales. In his first Annual Report the Director has this to say about the management of hospital services for the mentally handicapped.

"Many hospital staff have criticised their Regional Boards and the Department of Health for failing to provide a modern policy, plan modern provision, or indeed give the leadership needed in recent years. . . .

The visiting teams have found that Management Committees also vary considerably in their attitudes. Many are very conscientious and visit regularly, but often restrict their interest to the social activities or immediate physical conditions. In general, however, many seem fearful of innovation and tend to accept the matters put before them by the senior officials of the hospitals. It is rare to hear of a Management Committee asking about the organisation of the therapeutic services in the hospital, or for information which would confirm that the senior staff are working effectively together, or planning for the development of the therapeutic services. I hear that Management Committees are rightly concerned that they should not interfere with individual clinical judgment or with professional decisions in general. On the other hand, they seem unduly fearful of showing any interest or concern over the way the therapeutic services are developing or the general pattern of care or therapeutic atmosphere within the hospital as a whole.

One conclusion to be drawn from the teams' visits is that one of the most serious defects in the hospital services for the mentally handicapped lies in the failure of the senior medical, nursing and administrative staff to meet together to discuss the services provided by the hospital and to plan together for the future. Many hospitals fail to plan the therapeutic resources at their disposal so as to use them to best effect for the population concerned. It has frequently proved necessary to advise that some kind of multi-disciplinary planning committee should be formed to ensure that all the therapeutic groups meet and agree on a co-ordinated plan for the hospital. Some hospitals have been successful with planning committees including all heads of departments and representatives of ward staff. . . .

It is difficult to convey to those who have no experience of the problems, the stress imposed on ward staff. For example, two nurses may be responsible for rousing, dressing and toiletting 50 or so severely handicapped patients, most of whom cannot dress themselves without some help, and many are incontinent or become so with minimum waiting. In this situation there may be only two toilets available in the dormitory area. The same ward may have no room for occupational or social therapy, the hospital departments concerned may be too small and none of the patients may leave the ward from one week to the next. These conditions are the fault of management at all levels, not of ward staff, and the latter are understandably resentful of criticism they have sometimes received."

116. But he also says:

" We have found ample evidence of good practices and new ideas in every aspect of the hospital service for the mentally handicapped. At Regional Board level significant contributions to the development of the hospital services for the mentally handicapped have been apparent. . . .

The beneficial effects of Management Committees have also been apparent. In particular, in Wales the team were impressed by the attitude of the Management Committee and staff of a chest hospital which had agreed to accept a group of mentally handicapped patients although the hospital had had no experience of such patients in the past. There seemed little doubt that the interest and enthusiasm of the Management Committee had played a significant part in making a success of this new venture. At another hospital which had had serious difficulties, the beneficial influence of a recently appointed Chairman and interested Management Committee was apparent at all levels of the hospital's activities.

The teams have noted the widespread benefits which follow when a consultant involves the other therapeutic professions in day-to-day work, assessment and continuing treatment. They have noted the benefits which follow once he provides an increasing service within the community, particularly in out-patient clinics or in meeting parents' groups. In view of the fact that the amount of time a consultant can give to each

25

individual patient is limited, the most effective services have often been those where the consultant takes particular care to see that he enables other therapeutic professional staff to play their full role. . . .

Teams have seen nurses who take an active part in social training, help to place their patients in suitable situations in the community, and run an effective follow-up service for their patients. On wards, morale is often significantly higher where the ward nurse has a major say in the pattern of care in the ward, ward design and decoration, and the right to take relevant decisions for the individual patient. In the better hospitals it is usual to find that the ward staff have a good relationship with visiting relatives and are able to give them information on progress. . . ."

117. In the quality of management, as in most other aspects, standards vary widely from one hospital to another.

General comment on hospital services

118. Fundamentally, what has happened is that outdated views have continued to influence the allocation of financial and other resources to many hospitals for the mentally handicapped. In some places attitudes have not kept pace with new knowledge about the latent capacities of the mentally handicapped, public expectations of better services and the general rise in the standard of living. Too little account has been taken of the increasing burden placed on the hospital staff by changes in the make-up of the patient population.

119. But these generalisations are unfair if they give the impression that standards are low everywhere. Despite the difficulties outlined in this Chapter some hospitals provide a very high standard of care indeed for mentally handicapped patients. Almost all hospitals have some good features. Average standards compare well with those in many other developed countries. Within the hospitals forward-looking ideas abound. The fact that so much has been achieved with such inadquate resources is a tribute to the staff, and in particular to the nurses, on whom the deficiencies weigh most heavily, and on whom criticism has often been unfairly focused.

Success in rehabilitation of patients

120. Finally, it should be made clear that these hospitals do not have a wholly static population. In spite of the lack of residential homes outside, and the problems inside, the hospitals have succeeded in rehabilitating and discharging patients in all age-groups, including children and the elderly.

121. Relevant figures are given in Table 4. They relate to the total numbers in hospital in Table 2 (paragraph 84), but exclude patients admitted for short-term care of less than three months who, though they now account for well over half the admissions each year, occupy only about 3 per cent of the beds at any one time.

122. Between 1954 and 1964 there was a substantial increase both in admissions and discharges. Both have fallen slightly since 1964. Even with the present very limited facilities for care outside hospital, particularly residential accommodation, one patient in every twenty is discharged each year; of these about half are discharged within two years of admission. About a third of all discharges take place after more than five years in hospital. More patients leave the hospitals each year through discharge than through death.

26

TABLE 4

Admissions and discharges and length of stay in hospitals or hospital units for the mentally handicapped, exluding patients staying less than 3 months

	Age 0–14				15–34				35–54				55 and over				Total			
	1954	1964	1968	1969	1954	1964	1968	1969	1954	1964	1968	1969	1954	1964	1968	1969	1954	1964	1968	1969
Admissions	1,221	1,511	1,580	1,367	1,146	2,422	2,201	2,081	399	1,241	769	821	72	289	315	329	2,838	5,463	4,865	4,598
Discharges	n.a.	426	446	437	n.a.	1,951	1,615	1,618	n.a.	822	611	707	n.a.	218	286	241	1,239	3,417	2,958	3,003
Deaths ...	n.a.	123	151	124	n.a.	228	238	268	n.a.	235	291	331	n.a.	453	607	620	748	1,039	1,287	1,343
Length of stay before discharge:																				
3 months– 2 years	n.a.	249	301	269	n.a.	996	897	853	n.a.	270	224	234	n.a.	45	63	49	127	1,560	1,485	1,405
2–5 years	n.a.	78	87	102	n.a.	436	338	335	n.a.	137	96	102	n.a.	21	36	34	253	672	557	573
5 years or more ...	n.a.	99	58	66	n.a.	519	380	430	n.a.	415	291	371	n.a.	152	187	158	859	1,185	916	1,025
Total ...	n.a.	426	446	437	n.a.	1,951	1,615	1,618	n.a.	822	611	707	n.a.	218	286	241	1,239	3,417	2,958	3,003

n.a. = not available.

134511

E* 2

CHAPTER 5

THE SERVICES REQUIRED

123. The main principles on which, according to current thinking, services for the mentally handicapped and their families should be based were summarised in Chapter 3. The description of present services in Chapter 4 shows how far we are from applying them fully. The present Chapter describes in more detail the component parts of the services we should now aim to provide. Chapter 6 describes the action in hand or needed to achieve this, and Chapter 7 the important contribution which voluntary service can make.

Collaboration between authorities and between professions

124. The mentally handicapped and their families need help from professions working in services administered by a variety of authorities and departments. It is important that the resources of the health services, personal social services and education services should be deployed in close and effective collaboration. Only if this is done can the relevant professional skills be most effectively used to provide complete and co-ordinated services.

Main services required

125. The main services required are:

(i) Prevention or early detection of mental handicap so far as practicable.

(ii) Comprehensive assessment of the mentally handicapped person's assets and disabilities, and periodic reassessment.

(iii) Co-ordinated advice, support and practical help for their families.

(iv) Education, social and work training, day care and occupation or the opportunity for work according to the handicapped person's individual capacities.

(v) Residential accommodation according to individual needs.

(vi) Hospital medical, nursing and other services for those who require them, as out-patients, day patients or in-patients.

Prevention and early detection
Limited but increasing knowledge

126. At present the possibilities of preventing mental handicap are very limited. The principal methods at present available are described in the Appendix. Most of these are quite recent and not yet widely applied, and most are at the research stage.

127. Genetic counselling with family planning advice and treatment have preventive possibilities. Research is still being carried out into the early antenatal detection of Down's syndrome (mongolism). Expert care during labour has been shown to reduce the incidence of handicaps associated with the hazards of birth. Evidence is becoming available to show that intensive care for babies can lower the incidence of handicaps after birth.

128. Regular developmental screening of young children, particularly those at special risk, is essential to detect as early as possible deviant mental development.

129. There is evidence that mild degrees of mental handicap among culturally deprived children can be improved by pre-school education and by help for their families.

Organisation for prevention and detection

130. It is important that these preventive measures (and others which may become available as research increases our knowledge of the causes of mental handicap) should be known and used. Doctors and nurses in general practice and domiciliary health services and in hospitals should all be concerned with this, as should social workers and others who are in touch with parents or prospective parents. A co-ordinated organisation is needed to achieve this; it should include a reliable recording system to help in keeping under review all children at risk of developing mental or physical handicaps.

Comprehensive assessment

Multi-disciplinary approach

131. As soon as any defect is detected or suspected, a comprehensive assessment of the nature of the handicap or handicaps, and of the needs and problems of the handicapped person and his family, is required. Medical, educational, psychological and social aspects should be considered together, as appropriate to the age of the child. No one person can be expected to possess the range of skills required; a multi-disciplinary approach is needed. Multi-disciplinary assessment should be repeated at intervals, as the handicapped child or adult grows and develops. The members of the assessment team will vary according to the handicapped person's age and current problems.

Assessment and reassessment

132. When mental handicap is detected or suspected in a young child, important members of the assessment team will be a paediatrician concerned in the assessment and care of handicapped children, a consultant in psychiatry, and other experts in medicine, education, psychology, nursing and social work. The family doctor should always be involved as well as others concerned with support for the family, such as the health visitor and social worker. Reassessment of progress should be made frequently during childhood.

133. As the child grows older, educational and social assessment become increasingly important. Handicapped adolescents and adults need special assessment of their vocational and social capacities and skilled advice on employment; this should be arranged for every young person well before he or she leaves a special school.

134. Mentally handicapped adults should be examined and assessed regularly, whether they are living at home, in another residential home,

or in hospital. The assessment should be directed particularly to their medical condition, social capacity, the extent to which their needs are being met and their potentialities developed, and whether progression to other forms of care is needed. Regular assessment should form part of the programme of adult training centres and sheltered workshops.

Organisation for assessment

135. Arrangements for setting in train the initial assessment of newly detected handicap, and subsequent reassessment, should be agreed locally by all concerned. The different needs of children at various stages of development, and of adolescents and adults, must be taken into account in drawing up a plan of action. This should be known to all who may be the first to suspect mental handicap or be involved in the care of mentally handicapped children or adults. These include general practitioners; psychiatrists, paediatricians and others working in hospitals; doctors, health visitors and others in the community health services; social workers and others in the personal social services; and staff of the education services and special employment services.

136. Effective co-ordination is essential. Methods of achieving it need further study. The Department of Health and Social Security hopes to issue guidance on this in relation to the comprehensive assessment of persons with any form of handicap or disability.

137. Special comprehensive assessment centres for handicapped children (of any age or handicap) are essential, on the lines recommended in the memorandum on hospital services for children issued by the Department with HM (71) 22. This does not necessarily require new buildings, though in some places an addition to an existing building may help.

138. A multi-disciplinary team can also meet in a health centre, an out-patient clinic, an adult training centre, a special school, a residential home or a hospital, whichever is most convenient and appropriate for discussing the assessment and progress of individual children or adults.

Advice and practical help for the family

Counselling

139. When handicap is first detected, the parents must be told this sympathetically and skilfully. They need help in understanding the nature of their child's handicap, an experienced view of what to expect from the child and of the likely family problems as he grows older, and advice on how the family itself can best help the handicapped child to develop his abilities to the full. They also need a realistic appraisal of the services available, including voluntary services, and information on how to obtain them. If there is a co-ordinated multi-disciplinary approach to assessment there should be no risk of parents receiving conflicting advice.

140. Parents also need help with problems of adjustment arising from their own feelings towards a handicapped child, such as disappointment, sense of failure, anxiety about the future and concern for any other children

in the family. These personal difficulties can lead for example to rejection of the handicapped child on the one hand, or over-protection on the other, either of which may have a lasting effect on the child's future. The advice given to parents should take into account the total family situation including the needs of other children so as to avoid subjecting them to deprivation or undue strain as a result of the preoccupation of their parents with the handicapped child.

141. Many people including general practitioners, health visitors, social workers, psychiatrists and paediatricians, have a contribution to make in advising parents, but their work must be co-ordinated. As the child grows older his teachers and others concerned with his treatment or training should also contribute. The person best placed to act as co-ordinator is likely to be the social worker, who should take her part in the multi-disciplinary team as soon as handicap is suspected and thereafter maintain a continuing relationship with the handicapped child and his family.

142. Many parents obtain relief and reassurance from contact with other parents of mentally handicapped children. The establishment of local parents' groups in some areas has proved a valuable support.

Practical assistance

143. The family will also need practical assistance of many kinds. This may include home help, domiciliary nursing, laundry service for the incontinent, sitters-in, play centre, day nursery, nursery school, youth club, and temporary residential care for the handicapped person during emergencies or holidays. Voluntary as well as statutory service will help, and may need to be invoked and co-ordinated by the social worker. Services needed for education, training, care and treatment during the day are described later in this Chapter.

144. Some families may also qualify for the new tax-free attendance allowance of £4·80 per week which will be available from December 1971 under Section 4 of the National Insurance (Old persons' and widows' pensions and attendance allowance) Act 1970, where a severely disabled person at home requires care or attention day and night, or continual supervision for his own safety or that of others.

The family as a whole

145. The family should be told about these services and advised on their use. This requires skilled evaluation of the real needs of the family, particularly of the mother. Reassurance and personal guidance from the health visitor and social worker on how to care for her child herself may at times be more valuable to the mother than bringing in help from outside. At other times, however, in the interests of her own health and that of the rest of the family, a period of total relief from the daily routine of caring for the handicapped child or adult may be necessary. Caring for a mentally handicapped person at home makes great calls on the family's emotional reserve. The essence of good community care is the availability of someone, usually the social worker, from whom they can confidently expect understanding and help to meet any situation.

Leaving the family home

146. If and when the time comes for the handicapped person to leave the family home and enter residential care or hospital for more than a temporary stay, this should be planned well in advance so as to cause the least possible distress to the family and upset to the handicapped person. The full co-operation of the family will be needed to help him to settle in his new environment. Ideally, this will be close to his family home. But if it is not, additional practical help may be called for in the form of transport, or sitting-in services for other children to allow the parents to visit. Extra help may be needed in the home when the handicapped person comes home for weekends or for a longer holiday. The tax-free attendance allowance mentioned in paragraph 144 will be payable if the circumstances justify it, either for the full week(s) of the holiday or on a daily basis if the severely handicapped person is at home for less than a week at a time.

Education for children

Pre-school

147. Mentally handicapped children need the stimulus of companionship with other children and adults. Recent research has demonstrated the value of an early start to the slow process of social training and education. This can begin in the diagnostic or assessment centres run by some local education authorities, in nursery schools, in special classes, in the special schools hitherto called junior training centres or in day nurseries or playgroups. Very severely handicapped children may benefit by going each day to a hospital if the family can manage to provide the necessary care at other times. Any of these arrangements not only benefits the child; it also frees the mother for some hours each day.

Change in responsibility for education

148. On 1 April 1971 local education authorities became responsible for the education and training of all mentally handicapped children. The " junior training centres " previously provided by local health authorities are now run by local education authorities as separate special schools for educationally subnormal children, apart from a very few centres for which some other form of educational organisation has been considered appropriate. Local education authorities are also now responsible for the education of all children in hospital.

149. Already, before this transfer, many of the practices typical of normal education have been assimilated in training centres and hospitals. The value of play and exploration is recognised. Many classrooms offer a variety of learning situations arranged by the teacher to meet the needs of individual children, who learn less readily than normal children do from free activity methods. Emphasis is given to social adaptation and language development, to teaching each child to be as independent as possible and to behave in a socially acceptable way.

150. Mentally handicapped children develop at different rates. At 16 some may still be very immature, needing the atmosphere and approach of the school for a further year or so. Others may be sufficiently mature to

transfer to an adult centre where they will be treated as young adults, given an increasing measure of responsibility and be prepared more consciously for the world of work. For some the transition may need to be in stages so that the young person can gradually gain confidence in the new environment. In any case, careful preparation must be made for the transition by introducing pupils at school to a wide range of manual and creative skills, and for coming to terms with the everyday world outside the school.

Benefits of the change

151. The education service will build on the foundations laid by the health and hospital services. Three of the main benefits expected from the change are the availability of educational advice, fuller professional training for the staff, and flexibility in placing children who up to now have been on the borderline between the education and health authorities.

152. Children with severe mental handicap will no longer be excluded from the educational system, and it should become easier for those in hospitals to attend special schools in the community together with children living at home. New special schools in the community should be planned with this dual intake in mind. Such intermingling of children will become increasingly practicable as fewer children are admitted to large isolated hospitals and more to the smaller units in centres of population as recommended later in this Chapter. At the same time, within hospitals arrangements will be made to provide education for those heavily handicapped children who in the past have often been denied education for lack of a " school " in the hospital or of teaching staff to visit them in the wards.

Special care

153. The functions of special care units, for children and for adults, and the scope for their development were described in paragraphs 62–63. The best arrangements need to be worked out in consultation by local education authorities, the local authorities' health and social services departments and the hospital authorities. Joint arrangements may be needed, especially for adults.

Social and work training, occupation and further education for adults

Need for special training and occupation

154. Most mildly handicapped school-leavers are able to go directly into open or sheltered employment, possibly with special help from the Youth Employment Service. Some need a period of special training in an adult training centre first. Most of the severely handicapped also need to attend an adult training centre; some may proceed from this to sheltered or open employment, but the majority need permanently some form of work or occupation specially geared to their limited capabilities.

155. The object of this special training and work or occupation is to develop work habits and to increase self-reliance generally, so as to help each handicapped person to live a more independent life. The programme should include further education and facilities for social and recreational

33

activities. Much of the work needs to be simple and repetitive or capable of being broken down into simple elements, but some mentally handicapped people obtain quite a high degree of skill which allows more sophisticated processes to be introduced.

Organisation

156. Local authorities are responsible for providing these services for the mentally handicapped who live with their families or in other residential homes. All mentally handicapped patients in hospital need similar services, and many may benefit from coming out of the hospital daily to join others in the local authorities' adult training centres. In some places, handicapped people not living in hospital may go to industrial or occupational training units in the hospital. There is scope for considerable joint use of services.

157. Full use should also be made of services which though not provided primarily for the mentally handicapped can make a valuable contribution to meeting their needs. For those who are capable of remunerative employment there are the services of the Department of Employment, viz.:

(i) The service of Disablement Resettlement Officers in finding suitable employment, mainly in ordinary industry but if necessary in special workshops under sheltered conditions (see (ii) below). They can also advise local authorities and hospitals on the sort of jobs which are available locally, and in suitable cases arrange admission to an industrial rehabilitation unit (see (iii) below).

(ii) Sheltered workshops are provided, with financial help from the Department of Employment, nationally by Remploy Limited, locally by local authorities, and for special classes of people by voluntary bodies. Their purpose is to provide work for disabled people who though capable of making a significant contribution are unlikely because of the severity of their disability to obtain employment under ordinary conditions.

(iii) Industrial Rehabilitation. The Department of Employment operate industrial rehabilitation units to provide for disabled people preparation for return to work and assessment as to the most suitable form of employment. The facilities are available to people with mental handicap who need preparation for return to work. Some workshops run by voluntary organisations and one run by a local authority are recognised by the Department of Employment as providing, on an agency basis, industrial rehabilitation for people with mental handicap. These workshops receive some financial assistance from the Department of Employment.

Residential accommodation

A local authority responsibility

158. If and when a mentally handicapped child or adult has to leave his family home, a suitable substitute home must be provided. Some will need to go to hospital because of physical handicaps or behaviour problems that require special medical, nursing or other skills. The local authorities have a statutory duty to provide residential care for all others, and also for those who can leave hospital after a period of treatment there.

34

Various forms

159. Residential care may be with foster parents, in lodgings, ordinary housing or a group home or flatlets with social work support, a children's home, a home for the elderly mentally infirm, or a home (local authority or voluntary) specifically for mentally handicapped children or adults. The choice depends on the age, handicap and degree of social independence of each handicapped person.

160. To give scope for progress to lesser or greater support as time goes on, each local authority should provide a range of choice. A recent and useful trend is to have a small residential home with flatlets or a group home nearby, or even in the same building structure. This makes progress to lesser support possible without uprooting the handicapped people from the community they know and cutting their links with familiar friends.

Homes not hostels

161. The term "home" is deliberately used in this Paper in preference to "hostel", which is usually used at present. The word "hostel" has the ring of impermanence and a certain austerity. It usually describes a place where people stay while working or studying, away from their home. But residential homes for the mentally handicapped are a permanent substitute family home for most of the residents, even though they keep in touch with their own families and visit them as often as possible. The staff and residents become a substitute family group. The home should be homely.

162. In fact most of the present local authority "hostels" do have this homely atmosphere. It is better to call them "homes" when a generic term is needed. Each should normally be known by its own individual name, or street number, as any other house is.

163. Homes of this kind will supply much of the residential care needed. They should be small, and usually have residents of both sexes. For adults, 25 is now normally the maximum for a single home, and 20 the maximum for children; many may be smaller. Most adults should have single rooms, and no rooms have more than four beds. Plenty of space for recreation is needed, indoors and outside. Residents should use local parks and sports grounds, and shops. In such surroundings a family atmosphere can be created, where individuals can develop within a small group and with their own interests and possessions.

Personal relationships

164. Personal relationships between the handicapped child or adult, the family he has just left, and the new foster parent or landlady or staff of the residential home are very important. The mentally handicapped need the security which comes from the personal interest of people they know and trust. Contacts with their own family or with social workers they already know should therefore be maintained, and a new lasting relationship formed with the people in their new substitute home.

165. Anyone chosen to look after the mentally handicapped must be a person able to establish such lasting relationships, but not be over-protective. Given someone to turn to for help with problems of ordinary life many mentally handicapped people can achieve considerable independence but this has to be positively encouraged.

166. Social workers should work with the family and with the staff of the residential home, the foster-parent or landlady. They should also be in contact with other people as need arises, *e.g.* the teacher, the manager of the training centre, the employer, the Disablement Resettlement Officer, the club leader or voluntary worker.

Personal help

167. In future, when only those really requiring hospital care are admitted to hospital, local authority homes will receive residents in need of more personal care and help than most present residents. These will include people who require some help in feeding, washing or dressing themselves, or have minor emotional problems, or who might come to harm if not escorted when they go out. Older as well as younger children and even some adults may have occasional incontinence. This does not go beyond the type of personal attention which local authorities are accustomed to provide in children's homes and homes for the elderly.

Activities

168. Most residents should go by day to a special school, to an adult training centre or to some other occupation or employment outside the home. They should also be encouraged to do the sort of household jobs people normally do in their own homes. In every way, their activities should be as nearly the same as those of people in a normal home environment as their handicaps permit.

Weekly boarders

169. In addition to permanent residents, places in residential homes are also needed for children and adults who live too far away from a special school or adult training centre for daily travel and will wish to spend five days a week, going home at week-ends.

Short-term care

170. Homes should also be ready to provide short-term care for other mentally handicapped children and adults in emergencies or to give those with whom the handicapped person is living an opportunity for a holiday. This is a vital factor in enabling families to keep a mentally handicapped relative at home; it applies also to foster parents and to landladies. To some extent the demand is seasonal; some homes specially for holidays, open for only part of the year, may be useful.

Patients disharged from hospital

171. It is the responsibility of the local authority social services department to provde any social work support needed for patients after discharge from hospital, and where necessary to find them suitable residential accommodation. This should be done in consultation with the hospital staff. In some areas hospital staff at present have to find lodgings or residential employment for patients who are ready for discharge but have no home to go to. Such arrangements may not be successful unless accompanied by social work support, which the local authority social worker should provide. She will usually be better placed, too, through her local knowledge, to find

suitable landladies or arrange admission to a local authority home or to a private or voluntary home registered by the authority. The local authority's general duties for the care of the mentally handicapped enable them to make a financial contribution towards the cost of accommodation, including lodgings, which hospitals have no power to do.

The elderly

172. Table 2 in paragraph 84 shows the large increase in recent years in the number of people over age 55 in hospitals for the mentally handicapped. Table 4 at the end of Chapter 4 shows that increasing numbers are being admitted when already aged 55 or over, and considerable numbers discharged. Many of these probably require residential rather than hospital care. Local authorities need to consider what services they should be providing for the growing numbers of elderly mentally handicapped people.

173. At present, no special provision is made for this group and our information about them is sketchy. But relevant information will soon be available from the censuses mentioned at the end of Chapter 2. These will tell us the number in different age groups at present in hospital and in residential homes, and the severity of their handicap(s) and other characteristics. With this information it should be possible to estimate the number of elderly mentally handicapped people for whom services should be planned.

Hospital services
Treatment not residential care

174. At present, for reasons explained in Chapter 4, hospitals are used as homes for many who, when admitted, really required residential care of the sort described in paragraphs 158 to 173. As local authority services develop, this should cease.

175. There are different opinions, even among the experts, on the extent to which local authority services can meet the needs of people with substantial but not profound mental handicap, with or without associated physical handicap, and on the extent to which such people require medical, nursing or other skills which it is the function of hospitals to provide. As the local authority services develop, this will become clearer. The rest of this Chapter assumes that many will require hospital services, as out-patients, day-patients or in-patients, and that some can best be served by a combination of local authority and hospital services. Tentative estimates of the numbers of mentally handicapped people requiring various services are given at the end of the Chapter.

General services to be used

176. When a mentally handicapped person requires hospital treatment for a physical illness, or surgery, or treatment for mental illness, he should normally receive this in the appropriate department of a general or mental illness hospital. There may however be cases where psychiatric treatment for a mental illness associated with severe mental handicap, or occasionally treatment for physical illness, is better provided in a hospital or unit accustomed to dealing with the severely mentally handicapped.

Hospitals' contribution to prevention, assessment and family counselling

177. Paragraphs 130 to 141 mention the need for hospital staff to participate in the prevention, early detection and comprehensive assessment and reassessment of mental and other handicaps. Children's departments of general hospitals have an important part to play in diagnosis and assessment and early remedial measures. Psychiatric out-patient clinics in local hospitals are also useful for this purpose. The contacts thus established between hospital psychiatrists and handicapped children or adults and their parents also help to support the family while the handicapped member lives at home, and to ease the transition to hospital if he needs to be admitted later.

Day hospital services

178. Day hospital services are needed for handicapped children or adults who can live at home but need assessment in a hospital setting. They are also required for some of those with severe physical handicaps or behaviour problems whose families can keep them at home if relieved of their care for a few hours each day. For such patients day services may replace or postpone in-patient admissions, or allow discharge after a period as an in-patient.

179. Day patients may attend hospitals which also treat in-patients, or separate day hospitals. Any hospital taking day patients must of course be easily accessible to the population it serves. For some patients relatively simple accommodation will suffice, and may be in a small local unit. Others will need treatment facilities which can be provided only in a larger hospital. In addition to whatever medical, nursing and other specialist services are needed, there must be facilities in the hospital or nearby for education for children and suitable occupation and training for adults, and also meals and recreation. Paragraph 63 refers to the possibility of associating day hospital services in some areas with a training centre or special school provided by the local authority.

In-patient treatment

180. In-patient services are needed for those who can no longer remain in the family home or in other residential care and require treatment or training under specialist medical supervision or constant nursing care. A high proportion will need this because their mental handicap is associated with severe physical disability or behaviour disorder.

181. The aim is to help all patients, including the most severely handicapped, to develop to their full potential and to achieve as positive and independent a life as their handicaps allow. After a period of treatment or training some will be able to be discharged back to life in the community with support from the local authorities or hospital out-patient or day-patient services.

Staff for positive therapy

182. The hospitals should be staffed to provide all necessary medical, dental and para-medical services. In addition to doctors, dentists and nurses, this may require, according to individual patients' needs, the services of whole-time or part-time psychologists, physiotherapists, speech therapists

and other specialists. A range of educational services for patients of all ages should be provided by or in consultation with the local education authority, together with industrial and occupational therapy and a range of leisure activities for which appropriate staff need to be employed.

Management of co-ordinated therapeutic programmes

183. The hospital management, through its chief officers, should provide for the co-ordination of therapeutic programmes. All those concerned with patients should contribute to this, including teachers and instructors, occupational and other therapists as well as doctors, nurses and professional administrators. Efforts now being made to encourage this are described in Chapter 6.

Home in hospital

184. Whether a patient stays in hospital a relatively short time or a long time the hospital becomes in effect his home as well as a place of treatment. The conditions and general atmosphere should be as homelike as possible, with every appropriate stimulation through education, industrial or occupational therapy and leisure activities, and personal possessions for every patient. If staff are allocated to care for small groups of patients, individual attention can more easily be given and personal relationships established. The principles mentioned in paragraphs 161 to 166 and in 168 apply in hospitals just as much as in residential homes.

Contacts with the family

185. Admission to hospital should have no air of a final break with the patient's family, as it often has at present. The hospital staff should be at pains to ensure that their own professional services do not make the relatives feel superfluous, nor guilty at shedding their immediate responsibility for the handicapped person. A family's inability to carry on caring for a severely handicapped child or adult should not be seen by them as a failure, or as an occasion for them to withdraw their interest. The points mentioned in paragraph 146 apply in this situation.

186. If the hospital employs its own social workers, they should maintain close links with the local authority social services departments to ensure a continuing service to families while their relative is in hospital, and to secure proper arrangements if and when he is discharged. Another possible arrangement is for the local authority to provide a social work service, used jointly with the hospital, for patients from the authority's area and their families; the same social workers would then be responsible whether or not the handicapped member of the family becomes a hospital in-patient. If a hospital in-patient has no family links, the local authority social worker can provide a contact with the community; this may be particularly necessary if the patient is a child.

187. If contacts with the family are to be maintained, the hospitals must be accessible to the populations they serve. This will affect both the location and the size of hospitals or hospital units for the mentally handicapped, which are discussed in paragraphs 189 to 192 and in Chapter 6.

Contacts with the surrounding community

188. Contact should be maintained with life outside hospital through contacts with the local community around the hospital, as well as with patients' families. Voluntary help and visitors from the local community should be encouraged to come into the hospital. Patients should go out to shop, to use local parks and playgrounds and join in social events; even severely handicapped patients can benefit from the interest and stimulus this provides. Some may also go out of the hospital regularly to work or to attend adult training centres or special schools.

Size and location of hospitals

Different views

189. Most of the points made in paragraphs 176 to 188 are accepted in principle by those now concerned with hospital services for the mentally handicapped. But there are different opinions about the best size and location of hospitals or hospital units.

190. Some consider that there should be no separate hospitals of the present sort for the mentally handicapped, and that general hospitals should meet all the hospital needs of the population of the districts they serve, including the mentally handicapped. Thus mentally handicapped children would be looked after in units associated with the children's department, and mentally handicapped adults in small units at, or operationally linked with, the general hospital. Education, training and occupation for many of the patients would be provided in the training centres used by other mentally handicapped persons living in the community. It is argued that this is right in principle, would make it easier to recruit staff, would overcome problems of professional isolation, would help patients retain their links with the local population, would make it much easier for relatives to visit and would overcome the problems of a segregated community.

191. Others favour larger specialised hospitals as in the present hospital service, though not so large as to be extremely remote from most of their population. In such hospitals, they say, it is easier to provide a wide range of services for occupation, training and recreation. It is argued that only a hospital which brings together the mentally handicapped from a wide area can be large enough to classify patients with varying degrees or types of handicap, separate them in different wards and villas and provide the right tempo of life for each. It is also suggested that this type of hospital is necessary in order to allow staff to specialise in the care of the mentally handicapped and promote research into their problems and treatment.

The Government's view

192. The Government considers it premature to form a final view on these questions. Experience of various solutions is necessary to test the theories in practice. The Government is therefore encouraging alternative lines of development within the general principles mentioned in Chapter 3 and paragraphs 174 to 188. The action now being taken to achieve this is described in Chapter 6.

Scale of services required

193. As present services, described in Chapter 4, are a far cry from our current ideals, we have little practical experience on which to base estimates of the scale on which we need to develop the various component parts of a new system.

194. The surveys described in Chapter 2 are intended to help towards such estimates, but have their limitations. They record people known to the authorities to be mentally handicapped, and therefore do not measure unknown need. They also necessarily reflect the present pattern of services; improved services may change requirements.

195. Estimating the number of places required—for training or occupation, in residential homes, and in hospitals for day patients and in-patients—is a matter of judgment. Estimates, therefore, vary considerably even among those who have studied the subject closely. They are affected by the differences of opinion on the role of doctors and nurses mentioned in paragraph 175 and by different views on the pattern of hospital services mentioned in paragraphs 190–191. Any estimates made now as a basis for planning services will need to be adjusted in the light of experience and further research.

196. On this tentative and provisional basis, Table 5 sets out guidelines for the numbers of places of various kinds per 100,000 population, and overall for England and Wales, which seem likely to be needed if services were fully developed along the lines described in this Chapter. They take no account of expected population increase nor of longer survival of the severely handicapped.

TABLE 5

Planning figures for services for the mentally handicapped compared with existing provision

Type of service	Places for children (age 0–15)			Places for adults (age 16+)		
	Required		Provided	Required		Provided
	Per 100,000 total population	Total England and Wales 1969	Total England and Wales 1969	Per 100,000 total population	Total England and Wales 1969	Total England and Wales 1969
Day care or education for children under five ...	8	3,900	500*	—	—	—
Education for children of school age: In the community— (i) for children with severe mental handicap living in the community ...	56	27,400	} 23,400	—	—	—
(ii) for children coming by day from hospital	6	2,900		—	—	—
In hospitals— (iii) for in-patients ...	7	3,400	4,600	—	—	—
(iv) for day patients ...	6	2,900	200	—	—	—
Occupation and training for adults: In the community— (i) for adults living in the community ...	—	—	—	130	63,700	24,500
(ii) for adults coming by day from hospital	—	—	—	20	9,800	100
In hospitals— (iii) for in-patients ...	—	—	—	35	17,200	30,000*
(iv) for day patients ...	—	—	—	10	4,900	200*
Residential care in the community (including short-stay): (i) in local authority, voluntary or privately owned residential homes ...	10	4,900	1,800	60	29,400	4,300
(ii) foster homes, lodgings, etc.	2	1,000	100	15	7,400	550
Hospital treatment: (i) for in-patients ...	13	6,400	7,400†	55	27,000	52,100†
(ii) for day patients ...	6	2,900	200*	10	4,900	500*

* Estimated.

† NHS beds allocated to mental handicap.

CHAPTER 6

ACTION TO IMPROVE SERVICES

197. Our task is to reorganise and improve our services to meet the requirements outlined in Chapters 3 and 5. This requires sustained action over many years by local authorities, by hospital authorities and others in the National Health Service, by voluntary bodies and by central Government. This Chapter describes the programmes of action which have been started, what they will cost and how soon they should achieve their targets. It also emphasises the need for joint planning and co-ordination of progress between local authority and hospital programmes. The important role of voluntary services is discussed in Chapter 7.

Local authority services
New priority

198. No new policy is involved for local authority services. What is needed is faster progress to overcome the present deficiencies. This will require money and more trained staff. The Government will play its part, but the main responsibility lies with the local authorities themselves. Faster development of their services is crucial, and must be a main task of their new Social Services Committees. Members and officers must meet the challenge of fulfilling their duty to provide a full range of services for the mentally handicapped in the community.

Targets

199. Table 5 at the end of Chapter 5 sets out for the first time quantitative targets for those parts of the local authority services which depend on buildings as well as on staff. It is not possible to set similar targets for increasing the numbers of social workers, home helps, play-group organisers and similar staff. The need for more such staff is great, but the mentally handicapped and their families are only one group among many for whom their services are required; any estimate of numbers related to the mentally handicapped alone would not be meaningful.

200. The figures in Table 5 are tentative. They must be tested in the light of experience, and adjusted to changes in population. But they give each local authority a clear provisional target for each of the services listed in the Table. In most cases these targets are far beyond what the authorities have yet planned to provide.

Expansion of residential homes and adult training centres

201. The services in which the greatest expansion is needed are adult training centres or sheltered workshops, residential homes for children and residential homes for adults.

Building targets

202. The target in Table 5 for adult training centres requires 43,500 more places in adult training centres than were in use or under construction in March 1971. A further 2,000 new places may be needed to replace

existing unsatisfactory buildings. Some 9,700 of these 45,500 places would be for hospital patients, for whom the hospital authorities would reimburse an appropriate share of running costs including loan charges; the running costs of 35,800 places in addition to those now in existence or under construction would fall to be met by the local authorities, with help from the rate support grant.

203. The Table 5 targets for residential homes for children and adults, excluding places in foster homes, lodgings, etc., require 2,800 more places for children and 24,100 for adults in addition to those now in use or under construction.

Capital investment and running costs

204. The capital cost of this number of additional places in residential homes and adult training centres would be about £154 million at 1970 prices. The annual running costs, including loan charges, falling on local authorities when these places and those now under construction are in use would be about £38 million (at 1970 prices) in addition to the cost of services of this sort in 1970–71, which was about £14 million. These figures include the cost of places in voluntary or private residential homes, but not of places in foster homes, lodgings, etc.

Rate of progress increasing

205. The pace of development of residential homes and adult training centres is already quickening. Capital investment in terms of projects started has risen from less than £1 million in 1959–60 to nearly £5·2 million in 1970–71, and is expected to reach £7 million in 1971–72.

206. The 1970–71 and 1971–72 figures reflect the added impetus given by the Government's policies and their decision in November 1970 to allocate £40 million additional capital and revenue resources to local authority and hospital services for the mentally handicapped for the four years 1971–72 and 1974–75, and by the agreements reached in the negotiations on rate support grant for the years 1971–73.

The next four years

207. In the four years 1971–72 to 1974–75, these resources and local authorities' present plans should allow building starts for nearly 10,000 new places in adult training centres, 750 new places in homes for children and 3,500 new places in homes for adults. New buildings would increase revenue costs during this period by an average of something under £2 million each year over the previous year at 1970 prices. This is slightly higher than the present annual increase which is likely in 1971–72 to exceed £1·5 million for the first time. The annual increase would rise progressively during the four-year period.

Completing the programme

208. Further progress will depend on what rate of development can reasonably be expected, taking into account the priority which these services deserve and the many other calls on resources. Bearing in mind the need to develop other services for the mentally handicapped, including social workers and other domiciliary services and education, and also the other

important services for which local authorities are responsible, it seems reasonable to envisage capital investment in residential homes for mentally handicapped children and adults and adult training centres rising by about 2 per cent a year for the next 10 years from the £7 million expected in 1971–72. On this basis capital investment should reach nearly £8·5 million a year at 1970 prices in 1981–82. Thereafter capital investment might continue at at least that level until the targets are reached. This would involve an annual increase in revenue costs of about £2 million each year.

209. At that rate of progress, we could expect to have in use or under construction by 1986–87 about 34,600 more places in adult training centres than are in use or under construction now, about 2,250 more places in residential homes for children and 18,600 more places in homes for adults. If the planning figures in Table 5 were still valid at that time, this would leave a need for some 11,000 more places in adult training centres, 550 places in homes for children and 5,500 places in homes for adults, subject to increase or decrease to take account of population changes; this might take up to five years to complete at the same rate of progress.

210. The Government must necessarily express targets and forecasts in national terms. This national forecast of progress covers a time-span long enough for every authority to build up its services to the level of the planning targets. But some authorities would move faster than others, and some whose present services are better developed have less far to go and could expect to reach their targets earlier—some even within 10 years. Individual authorities will need to work out their own programmes, and co-ordinate them with the redevelopment of hospital services for their areas. So far as the resources available for capital projects allow, the Government will try to help authorities to complete their programmes within the time-span they set themselves; where necessary, priority must be given where the need is greatest.

Expansion of other services

211. For the reasons explained in paragraph 199 quantitative targets cannot be set for the recruitment of social workers, home helps and other staff for domiciliary services for the mentally handicapped and their families. But some allowance must be made for their cost in any forecast of rate of progress in local authority services for the mentally handicapped. Increased use of foster homes, lodgings and sheltered housing, and increased day-care for children under five (for which planning figures are given in Table 5) must also be taken into account. In assessing reasonable rates of progress for the building of new adult training centres and residential homes in paragraphs 207 to 210, it has been assumed that as these other services develop up to £1 million additional revenue expenditure may need to be incurred in any one year, and on average expenditure will rise over the whole period by at least £0·5 million a year. The rate of development will depend on the possibility of recruiting certain types of staff such as home helps, or of finding suitable lodgings, the output of training programmes, and other factors some of which will be outside individual authorities' control.

212. Education services also need development. This is being planned by the education departments and local education authorities who have recently taken over this responsibility. Building programmes of

approximately £1 million a year were in progress at 1st April 1971, and will continue at least at this level while the integration with the services for special education proceeds and the full measure of the capital requirements are ascertained. Arrangements are already in hand for substantial increases in the provision for training of teachers of mentally handicapped children.

Co-ordination with hospitals

213. This is discussed more fully in paragraphs 264 to 274. Paragraph 273 asks each local authority, in consultation with the hospital authorities for their area, to fix a date after which the hospitals will not be expected to admit, from that local authority's area, any more people who need residential rather than hospital care. In some areas this date should be within the period of the first four-year programme. Discussions will be held with the local authority associations about fixing a final date when this will apply throughout the country. The main object of this is to prevent future misplacements. It would also contribute to the relief of overcrowding in the hospitals.

Staff recruitment and training

214. Shortage of staff, particularly trained staff, was mentioned in Chapter 4 as a limiting factor on the quality and further development of all parts of the local authority services for the mentally handicapped. It is essential that recruitment and training of staff for training centres and residential homes and of social workers should expand in parallel with the rest of the development programme. This will not be easy. Training schemes for staff of adult training centres and residential homes have not been established long enough yet to be well known gateways to a satisfying career. For some years to come methods of stimulating recruitment, as well as the extension of training, will be one of the most important tasks of the authorities' new social services departments and the new Central Council for Education and Training in Social Work.

Adult training centre staff

215. About 170 people are now qualifying each year for the Diploma in the teaching of mentally handicapped adults awarded by the Training Council for Teachers of the Mentally Handicapped. The Training Council are alive to the need to expand staff training to keep pace with planned development of adult training centres and also to meet the needs of hospitals.

Residential home staff

216. Specific training for the staff of residential homes, other than children's homes, has only recently started. Experience abroad, notably in Denmark, has shown how much trained staff can do to develop the potential of the mentally handicapped in residential care. As the expansion of such care is so important a part of our planning, it is essential to expand training facilities for staff as a matter of priority.

217. There are now an increasing number of courses in Colleges of Further Education for students wishing to work in residential homes, including homes for the mentally handicapped. A few university courses

in applied social studies provide options for students who wish to work in residential homes. Intensive in-service training for staff in post who find it difficult to take full-time professional courses has been encouraged both by the Central Council for Training in Child Care and by the Council for Training in Social Work. These Councils will soon be replaced by the new Central Council for Education and Training in Social Work, as the body responsible for all social work training. It will clearly need to consider a substantial and urgent development of full-time courses and in-service training.

Social workers

218. The main training for social workers in the mental health services is provided by postgraduate university courses in psychiatric social work, and the courses leading to the Certificate in Social Work awarded by the Council for Training in Social Work. Holders of the Certificate in Social Work do not all take up work in mental health.

219. At present over 100 psychiatric social workers qualify each year and considerable expansion is planned. Expansion of courses for the Certificate in Social Work has been rapid. In 1970–71 there were 18 two-year courses leading to the Certificate, and the first year intake had risen to 406 students. In addition one three-year course has started, and there are three one-year courses for older experienced staff of whom some 50 are at present in training. The new Central Council will need to expand these training facilities very considerably to meet the demands for trained social workers in all fields of social work.

Local authorities' programmes

220. One of the first tasks of the new social services department of each local authority will be to formulate a training programme for these and other staff. Each programme needs to include secondment to full-time courses and in-service training for each group of staff. The programme should allow for advance recruitment and secondment for training; for example it may be wise to select the person to be in charge of a new residential home and second him for training while the home is being built, so that he is qualified and ready to take up his duties as soon as it opens.

Hospital services

Comprehensive development programmes

Reorganisation

221. When local authority services are fully developed fewer hospital beds for mentally handicapped in-patients will be needed than we have now. But many will need to be in different places. New assessment and treatment facilities will be needed for out-patients, day patients and in-patients. Staff, buildings, equipment, furnishings and other essentials must be sufficient in quantity and quality to provide all patients with good treatment and good living conditions. For this, hospital services in each region need to be reorganised. Each Regional Hospital Board has been asked to work out a development programme to achieve this. The pattern of development is described in paragraphs 238 to 254.

Five-year programme of improvements

222. In some areas local authority services will not be fully developed for 15 years or more though they will be growing all the time with consequent relief to the hospitals. New hospital building will also take some time to plan and complete. In the meantime existing hospitals will continue to be used. A five-year programme to improve conditions in these hospitals is therefore in hand, as well as longer-term plans of reorganisation. This is described more fully in paragraphs 226 to 230.

Transitional measures

223. The hospitals contain many patients who when first admitted needed residential rather than medical or nursing care. As local authority services develop new admissions of this sort should cease, and more patients can be discharged from hospital.

224. Opinions differ on how many of those who have become institutionalised through long residence in hospital can be successfully rehabilitated and return to life in the general community. Some maintain that between a third and a half of all patients now in hospitals for the mentally handicapped could be discharged if residential and other facilities were available in the community. Others regard these estimates as far too high. Hospital Boards have been asked to include in their development programmes accommodation of a domestic character, within the hospital service, in which the possibility of rehabilitating institutionalised patients can be assessed in more normal living conditions.

Links between these

225. The longer-term, short-term and transitional measures are not separate, but parts of a co-ordinated programme. New units for day patients and in-patients which are provided early in the plans for reorganisation will also contribute to the five-year programmes by relief of overcrowding and of pressures on staff. So will some of the domestic-type units mentioned in paragraph 224; these are also likely to have a permanent place in the reorganised service. The raising of standards to a minimum acceptable level through the five-year programme of improvements will be of permanent benefit to those hospitals which will remain in use under the longer-term reorganisation. All these developments interlock.

Five-year programme of improvements

226. At the end of 1969 Regional Hospital Boards were given a list of "interim measures to improve hospital services for the mentally handicapped" and were asked to plan to achieve these within about five years starting in 1970–71. Some were expressed in terms of specific standards, others in more general terms. Some of the specific standards were minimum objectives, to be attained where the present conditions were worst, and were acknowledged to be less than the desirable standard. It was made clear that where standards were already higher, they should not be reduced to these levels.

227. These interim measures included the improvement of patients' food (to which the top priority was to be given) and clothing; minimum space standards and maximum numbers of patients in any one ward to

relieve the worst of the overcrowding; the provision of cupboards for all patients' personal possessions; specific minimum staff–patient ratios for doctors, dentists and nurses and minimum numbers of domestic staff related to the size of the hospital and the degree of dependency of the patients; recruitment of staff for other forms of treatment; upgrading of buildings and furnishings; and adequate staff accommodation.

228. They also included the establishment of regular discussions at ward level between doctors, nurses and other therapeutic staff, staff training schemes, the encouragement of voluntary service and where appropriate the employment of a full-time organiser of voluntary services.

229. The previous Government exhorted Boards to reallocate money within their total regional allocations for this purpose, made extra specific allocations totalling £3 million revenue in 1970–71, and reallocated £1 million capital in that year. They also indicated to Boards that further specific revenue allocations totalling at least £1½ million would be made for 1971–72.

230. The present Government has asked Boards to complete this programme of "interim measures". It has made available increased resources for the four years 1971–72 to 1974–75 for this programme and other developments for the mentally handicapped. From these increased resources the further specific revenue allocation for 1971–72 has been raised from the £1½ million promised by the previous Government to £3½ million.

Staff training and conferences

The special training project

231. The principal training need in the hospital service is reorientation of staff originally trained in an older tradition, and the interchange of new ideas and experiences. The programme of "interim measures" was accompanied by a special training project for this purpose. Its object is to help hospital staff now working with the mentally handicapped, both senior and junior, to understand the principles on which current policies are based, so that they will be able to take full advantage of the opportunities for more personal and positive patient care which the other parts of the five-year improvements programme should bring to their hospitals. Many of the nurses and other staff have longed for just such an opportunity. Ward staff in particular need more opportunities than they have been given in the past to widen their horizons, for example by exchanging ideas with other hospitals, and to develop their own ideas about ways in which they may give their patients a fuller life.

232. Most regions have appointed a special training project officer. Most of these are experienced nurses or administrators, who work closely with the Regional Training Officers. Following a training course for the project officers in July 1970 a great many activities are now under way. Regional conferences have been held to launch the scheme and multi-professional steering groups have been formed to guide the programme within the region. The training project concentrates first on improving communication within and between hospitals. Methods include seminars; working parties on subjects such as patients' clothing; inter-hospital visits; training for new staff; improved induction for newly recruited staff; attitude

surveys; and conferences and discussions to promote closer liaison with local authorities and voluntary services. Examples of good practice and of new methods of treatment have been publicised and brought to the notice of other hospitals.

Nurse training

233. The syllabus of training for the RNMS qualification has recently been reviewed by the General Nursing Council and a revised syllabus was published in November 1970. In compiling this syllabus the Council has had in mind the need to provide a training which gives a comprehensive insight into, and an understanding of, the problems of the mentally handicapped. The syllabus seeks to ensure that the nurse is fully conversant with all aspects of the care, education and training of the mentally handicapped both in the hospital and in the community. It is set out in broad terms to permit adaptations as necessary to meet changing needs.

234. A Committee under the chairmanship of Professor Asa Briggs is now considering the role, education and training of all nurses including those working with the mentally handicapped.

Refresher training

235. In order to maintain good standards, regular refresher training is necessary for qualified nurses and other professional staff. Regional Hospital Boards have been asked to give renewed attention to this as part of the improvements programme.

Multi-disciplinary management

236. At the same time the Department of Health and Social Security has taken the lead in encouraging new methods of co-ordinated management. Many hospitals have inherited a hierarchical staffing pattern with astonishingly little communication between different groups of staff—doctors, nurses, other therapeutic staff and the professional administrators. For effective management their work and objectives must be fully co-ordinated, within a general policy approved by the Hospital Management Committee. This implies the acquisition of new management skills.

237. Training conferences to assist this are being held by Regional Hospital Boards with the Department's help. Boards are to follow these up in consultation with senior staff in all their psychiatric hospitals.

Future pattern of hospital services

238. Paragraphs 189 to 192 mentioned differences of opinion about the best size and location of hospitals or hospital units for the mentally handicapped, and the Government's view that alternative lines of development should be encouraged in order to provide experience of different solutions.

239. Regional Hospital Boards have been told that their development programmes should provide for a range of assessment and treatment services for out-patients, day patients and in-patients on the lines described in Chapter 5, and that they should be based on the principles now set out in Chapter 3, points (xi) to (xiv) in paragraph 40 being particularly relevant to the planning of hospital services.

240. As to size and location of hospitals and hospital units, Boards have been asked to proceed on the lines described in the following paragraphs.

No new large hospitals

241. The best of the present hospitals, and others when improved by the relief of overcrowding, more staff, and better living conditions for patients, will give the necessary experience of large specialised hospitals with which to compare other solutions. No new hospitals of this type are therefore to be built for the time being, nor any hospitals of 500 beds or more enlarged. This is not intended to prevent the addition of facilities for education, occupational or industrial therapy or special treatment, but it is intended to prevent any increase in the number of in-patients.

242. New building to relieve overcrowding at hospitals with 500 or more patients on one site is to be located in areas of population elsewhere in the hospital's catchment area.

243. In hospitals with 500 or more patients on one site it may occasionally be necessary to provide very limited additional residential space for patients to allow existing wards to be vacated for upgrading. In such cases the erection on site of one system-built unit may be justified (provided it can be staffed).

New hospital buildings

Small or medium-sized units

244. New accommodation for in-patients will be provided either in units for the mentally handicapped within a hospital containing other departments as well, or in separate small or medium sized hospitals or hospital units. Each new hospital or unit will provide, or contribute to, a comprehensive range of in-patient, out-patient and day facilities for the mentally handicapped for a defined district. Such districts should not exceed about 250,000 population (possibly more in a densely populated area) and should generally coincide with the district served by one (or possibly two) general hospitals. These hospitals and units for the mentally handicapped will have close operational links with general hospitals serving the same district or with existing hospitals for the mentally handicapped.

245. Such hospitals or units will not contain more than 100–200 beds for in-patients (in addition to places for day patients) and many will be considerably smaller. The reason for this upper limit of 100–200 beds is that, on the planning figures in Table 5, 200 in-patient beds would eventually be necessary only for a population well in excess of 250,000; a hospital serving more people than this would be too remote from many of them.

246. Some of the smaller units will be for patients who, while requiring specialist medical supervision, are capable of going out daily to a special school or adult training centre or to employment, or patients with friends or relatives living nearby. These units should be homely in character, and preferably sited in a residential area. The living accommodation and social activities should be very similar to those in local authority homes as described in paragraph 163.

51

247. Other similar small units may be used for the purpose described in paragraph 224. For many patients such a unit will be a stepping-stone to discharge. Others may remain for longer periods.

Accommodation for adults

248. Long-stay accommodation for adults associated with general hospitals should not generally be actually on the general hospital site. There must be sufficient space for whatever occupational activities are needed by patients who do not go out from the hospital each day, and for leisure activities, and the buildings must be homely in character. This may be easier to achieve on a separate but nearby site. There may be an assessment and treatment unit in the general hospital.

Accommodation for children

249. New facilities for children will normally be separate from those for adults, have close links with the children's department of the general hospital and be provided in small domestic units. They may be either on or off the site of the general hospital. There may occasionally be situations where, by suitable planning, accommodation for children and adults can be provided in an acceptable way on one site, with separate living accommodation and other facilities for each age-group.

Education and work

250. Patients in any type of unit need facilities for education, social and work training and daily occupation. Arrangements may be made for some patients to attend nearby day hospitals, local authority special schools, training centres or sheltered workshops or to go out to other employment. For the rest, facilities are to be provided within the unit or at another hospital.

Recreation

251. All patients need recreational facilities. Those available to the general public, or provided for the handicapped outside the hospital, are to be used wherever appropriate, but living rooms and play-rooms and space for outdoor recreations will also be needed at every in-patient unit.

Teaching hospitals

252. Regional Hospital Boards have been asked to consult the undergraduate teaching hospitals in their regions about the contribution these hospitals will make to the reorganised hospital services for the mentally handicapped. Although most undergraduate teaching hospitals now accept responsibility for services for a defined district, in addition to their wider teaching functions, their services will not be complete until they include the full range of hospital psychiatric services, including out-patient, day patient and in-patient facilities for the mentally handicapped.

253. Several teaching hospitals, in and outside London, are actively planning units for the mentally handicapped. Some are beginning with assessment or treatment units for children, associated with their paediatric departments.

254.   As well as improving the teaching hospital's service to its district, this is important for the training of the future generations of doctors who will work in general practice or in hospital.   It should make them familiar with the problems of mental handicap as part of the wide spectrum of medicine.

Study of buildings

255.   Towards the end of 1969 the then Secretary of State for Social Services commissioned a study of buildings for the mentally handicapped by a team led by Mr. John Weeks.   This has been published and commended to hospital authorities.   As well as new design ideas it contains helpful comments on the effect of environment on the mentally handicapped, and suggestions for ways of adapting and re-furnishing old buildings to provide less impersonal and more stimulating conditions.

256.   The Department of Health and Social Security has produced standard designs for temporary buildings which can be erected quickly to relieve overcrowding by providing extra day-rooms or bedrooms, or for use as " decanting wards " while permanent buildings are being upgraded.   These as well as other methods are evaluated in the Weeks' report.

257.   More recently, in March 1971, the Department has issued general advice to Hospital Boards on short-life building, the circumstances in which it may be preferred to permanent building and its limitations.

Finance for development programmes

Four-year programme

258.   In November 1970 the Government announced the allocation of £110 million additional resources for the years 1971–72 to 1974–75 for the health and personal social services in Great Britain.   About £40 million of this will be available for hospital and local authority services for the mentally handicapped in England and Wales.   Including this £40 million, about £100 million at 1970 prices is expected to be spent in these four years on improving hospital and local authority services for the mentally handicapped.

259.   On the hospital side, it is hoped that capital expenditure in these four years will reach about £30 million.   Revenue expenditure rose from about £48 million in 1969–70 to about £53 million in 1970–71 and is expected to reach around £65 million by 1974–75 at 1970 prices.   Much of the increased revenue will be spent on relieving intolerable conditions in the existing hospitals.

260.   This increased revenue expenditure, together with a large proportion of the capital expenditure, should enable hospital authorities to achieve the five-year programme of improvements which started in 1970–71.   As far as possible Boards will aim to relieve overcrowding by providing new units in centres of population where they will contribute to the long-term reorganisation of services.   Some capital must also be spent on adaptations to unsatisfactory buildings which may not have a permanent place in the longer term.   The capital available for these four years should also allow some development of assessment services and other new buildings for the locally based services of the future.   It will require careful judgment to

53

get a proper balance between expenditure on buildings which are likely eventually to be abandoned but must be improved to relieve present intolerable conditions, and expenditure on existing or new buildings with a longer future use.

Completing the programme

261. As local authority services increase and the numbers in hospital drop, during and after the first four years, the increased rate of revenue expenditure will provide higher standards in the hospitals through higher expenditure per patient. In the long run annual expenditure at about the level expected in 1974–75 may be sufficient if experience confirms the planning figures set out in Table 5.

262. At a rough estimate some £120 million to £130 million in capital at 1970 prices may be needed for long-term reorganisation and interim improvements. This estimate does not include the expenditure which may be needed to take account of increase in population and longer survival of the severely handicapped.

263. Capital expenditure averaging about £7$\frac{1}{2}$ million a year would complete the hospital reorganisation programme within about the same period as the local authority development programmes described in paragraphs 208 to 210. Progress will necessarily vary from one area to another, and must be co-ordinated with local authority development through joint plans as described in paragraphs 264 to 273.

Joint planning by hospital and local authorities

Co-ordination essential

264. Effective co-ordination of plans between Hospital Boards (and the future reorganised health authorities) and local authorities will be even more important in the future than it has been in the past. Some mentally handicapped children and adults should in future be able to live at home if the local authorities provide social work support and other domiciliary services and the hospital provides day patient facilities; neither will be sufficient without the other. Our new planning assumes that a considerable number of children and adults who are hospital in-patients will receive their education or work-training in schools or adult training centres provided by local authorities outside the hospitals. When children are educated in hospital—whether in a hospital school or on the wards—their education will be provided by the local education authority and close co-operation between them and the hospital will be essential.

265. Such joint use of services will only be possible if both the location and the timing of hospital and local authority developments are co-ordinated by effective joint planning.

Alignment of areas

266. In the past, efficient co-operation between hospitals and local authorities has been hindered by the widely different areas served by each. This obstacle will be greatly reduced by the reorganisation of local government and of the National Health Service which will bring their areas of responsibility into line.

267. Even before then progress can be made by reorganising services in such a way that hospitals serve smaller and more local populations. Small hospital units should fit easily into such a reorganisation. It is more difficult with the larger hospitals, some of which at present serve 10 or more local authority areas. The possibility of " sectorising " these must be considered—that is to say designating particular wards or other units for patients from one sector of the hospital's total catchment area, each with their own team of staff who would also be responsible for out-patient and other services for the population of that sector. It is important that Regional Hospital Boards and Hospital Management Committees should work out such arrangements in consultation with the local authorities as soon as possible. The eventual aim should be to achieve catchment areas for each hospital or part of a hospital which coincide with local authority boundaries, or are wholly within one local authority area.

Co-ordinated plans

268. Each Regional Board has already been asked to prepare a development plan for its region and to consult the local authorities in doing so. The publication of this Paper, with the planning figures in Table 5 and the various recommendations for joint organisation of assessment and joint use of other services, will make it possible—and essential—to produce for each area co-ordinated plans to which both hospital and local authorities will work.

269. Preliminary discussions are already taking place between the Department and Hospital Boards. These should be followed later this year by detailed discussions between each Board and each of the local authorities in its region.

Priorities for local authorities

270. The first target for the local authorities will be to develop their services for the mentally handicapped who are not already in hospital, to prevent future misplacements. This will be the first priority, but must be accompanied by some movement of patients from hospitals to local authority residential homes. Other discharges from hospital should continue as at present, and as time goes on an increasing number of patients will be able to move to local authority homes.

271. To prevent misplacements and to permit discharge it is not only residential homes which are required. Adult training centres and social work support for the family may be equally relevant. When an adolescent leaves a special school, the family may be able to keep him at home if a place in an adult training centre is available; without it, it might be impossible for the family to manage and misplacement in hospital might be the result. It may be practicable to discharge a hospital patient to live in lodgings if he can attend a sheltered workshop or adult training centre but not otherwise. Nevertheless, more residential homes are a prime necessity. A balanced programme for each area is needed.

272. Each local authority should prepare its programme in the light of the discussions with the Hospital Board mentioned in paragraph 269. The initial stages of each authority's programme should then be included in the

new 10-year development plans for the whole of their health and social services which authorities will be asked to draw up during 1972. Preparation of these development plans will require close and detailed collaboration with the hospital authorities.

Local dates to end misplacements

273. In drawing up this programme the aim should be to fix for each area as early a date as possible after which the hospitals will not be asked to admit any more people who need residential rather than hospital care. Different dates may be fixed for children and for adults. In some areas this date may be set within the period of the first four-year programme; in others it may have to be later. The Government propose to discuss with the local authority associations the fixing of a final date when this will apply throughout the country.

Pace of development

274. Paragraphs 208–210 and 258–263 suggest that we must think in terms of development programmes for local authority and hospital services lasting 15–20 years over the country as a whole. The rate of progress will vary from one area to another. Some local authorities and some hospital authorities are already near the planning targets for some or all of the component parts of the service. In such areas it may be possible to complete the service we want in about 10 years. Others are less well advanced now and will need longer to complete. But for all areas agreed development plans should be prepared without delay, and implemented as resources permit.

Testing of planning figures

275. As time goes on, it will become clearer whether the planning figures in Table 5 are sound, or need adjustment. It will also become possible to evaluate new patterns of hospital services, with units of different sizes, in comparison with each other and with the best of the present larger hospitals. The effects of population growth and of increased survival of the severely handicapped will need to be allowed for, and also the possible effects of positive education and social stimulation on the independence achieved by the present generation of mentally handicapped children. Theories must be put to practical test, and changed if experience proves them wrong.

Research

276. Evaluation of new patterns of service as they develop is already included in our expanding programmes of research; this must continue and increase. Chapter 8 summarises the past research which has had a profound influence on our present thinking on services for the mentally handicapped, the scope for further research, and some of the subjects covered in our present programmes.

CHAPTER 7

VOLUNTARY SERVICE

The contribution of the private citizen

Personal interest

277. Private citizens, as individuals or through voluntary organisations, can make a unique contribution to the welfare of the mentally handicapped and their families, over and above what even the best public services can provide. Neighbours and voluntary groups can offer personal interest and assistance which is valued and valuable simply because it is voluntary—freely offered, not in the course of paid employment, but as a simple expression of personal concern between one human being and another.

278. This is immensely important in preserving—or re-establishing—the personal contact with ordinary life without which the mentally handicapped living in hospital become institutionalised. For families with a mentally handicapped member living at home, and for the staff of residential homes and hospitals, it mitigates isolation and loneliness; it helps to keep them in active contact with their own local community, which is beneficial both to them and to the handicapped people in their care.

Parents' groups

279. Parents of mentally handicapped children and adults, and other members of such families, can make an especially valuable contribution. They have a natural interest, and in many places have been the first to start voluntary work for the mentally handicapped. They can help each other, and form groups to take an interest in the local hospital and local authority services. Often they form the nucleus of the hospital's League of Friends. Similar groups can usefully act as "Friends" to residential homes and adult training centres. Their interest should be welcomed and encouraged by the hospitals and local authorities.

Influencing public opinion

280. All such activities by groups of private citizens have an added value in their influence on local public opinion and on attitudes towards the mentally handicapped. They help to give the community at large a greater understanding of what mental handicap means, the problems of families with a mentally handicapped member, and how the local community can help.

Supplementing official services

281. Voluntary organisations also can, and do, provide services similar to those which the public authorities now aim to provide. Indeed, voluntary bodies and individuals have been the pioneers in this field, as in so many other social services. Over a period of at least a hundred years, individuals, local groups and national voluntary organisations interested in the mentally handicapped have seen unmet needs and led the way by starting to provide services and by influencing public opinion.

residential homes for the mentally handicapped, nursing homes, training centres and sheltered workshops, and training courses and conferences for local authority hospital staff. They sponsor research and mould public opinion. By constructive and relentless criticism they goad Governments and local authorities to improve the statutory services nationally and locally. In addition, they contribute greatly to improving the quality of life of the people cared for by those authorities.

Growth of voluntary service

283. In recent years there has been a surge in the amount and diversity of voluntary help for the mentally handicapped in hospital and in the community. But much more is needed. The activities described in this Chapter are only examples of what is already done in some places. Similar activities would be welcomed elsewhere. New volunteers will undoubtedly see new methods of helping.

Service by young people

284. Even as recently as ten years ago many would have thought twice about encouraging young people to visit hospitals for the mentally handicapped. Recently young people have come forward from schools, colleges and youth clubs, and as cadet members of the long-established voluntary organisations, and have proved that they are as well suited for voluntary service to the mentally handicapped as older people, both in hospitals and in the community. Indeed, young people may find it easier than older people to establish rapport and get on easy terms with the handicapped.

Voluntary service for hospitals

Link with the community

285. Voluntary services are indispensable for maintaining links between the general community and hospital patients and staff. This is particularly important for patients who stay in hospital for years—as many mentally handicapped patients do—and for staff of isolated hospitals, many of whom live in the hospital grounds and can become isolated and inward-looking.

286. Volunteers can come into the hospitals and contribute to their internal life. They can take patients out locally or for longer excursions or holidays. They can help relatives to visit and can visit patients who have no interested relatives of their own.

287. No hospital unit is too large or too small to need such help. When hospital services are reorganised into smaller units, as foreshadowed in Chapter 6, voluntary help in maintaining contacts with the surrounding community will still be essential. A small hospital unit or residential home can be as isolated as a large one if it has no visitors.

288. Voluntary service can be directed to groups of patients or to individuals, or to raising funds for amenities for patients generally or for

staff. All these are needed. Voluntary work should be planned in consultation with the hospital's staff. The appointment of a voluntary help organiser, as mentioned in paragraph 296, can improve the scope for co-operation.

Group activities and services

289. Activities for small groups of patients which can be organised and led by volunteers include games of all sorts, drama, music, painting, modelling, and other hobbies, play groups, horse-riding—to name but a few. Voluntary organisations run library services and hospital shops and canteens. A most valuable service is the organisation of transport to help relatives visit patients in hospitals which are not easy to get to.

290. Groups of patients can also be given opportunities to join in activities outside hospital. Holiday camps can be organised, or day-trips, shopping expeditions, visits to cinemas, fun-fairs, football matches and other sports. And perhaps best of all, invitations to people's own houses, singly or in small groups.

Friendship for individual patients

291. At least a third of the 60,000 patients who now live in hospital are never visited. Others have only occasional visits from relatives. To befriend an individual patient is one of the most worthwhile forms of voluntary service. It is also one of the most difficult. Many patients, particularly the more severely handicapped, have difficulty in communication. Lack of an early response can be discouraging; it takes time and patience to form a useful relationship.

Funds for amenities

292. Fund-raising was one of the earliest forms of voluntary service, and is still indispensible. Funds have been raised for amenities for patients such as swimming pools, social centres, hairdressing salons, toys, aquariums, budgerigars and other pets, record players, and colour television. Contributions to Christmas festivities are welcome, and Christmas and birthday presents for patients. Amenities for staff (such as a building for a staff club) have also been provided, and are much needed, especially in the older hospitals.

Help for isolated hospitals

293. The hospitals most in need of help may be geographically isolated and difficult to reach by public transport. The surrounding community may be small, so that the local volunteers are necessarily few, often belong to several organisations and are heavily committed. The large isolated hospitals serve very large populations; with interest and ingenuity it should be possible to stimulate voluntary services of one sort or another from many different parts of a large " catchment area ". Leaders of local communities served by such hospitals could encourage this, and it will become more meaningful when the large hospitals are organised in units each serving a particular area, as mentioned in paragraph 267.

294. Voluntary help is especially important for these hospitals, where many patients are far from their homes and relatives, and staff are short.

They need more volunteers to organise outings and excursions, to help in educational and recreational activities, to visit patients. Help at weekends and evenings is particularly important, when teachers, instructors and therapists are off duty.

New sources of voluntary help

295. The work of the established associations is being augmented by an increasing variety of other groups. School children raised money to buy roller skates for patients at one hospital, and went to the hospital every weekend to help the children to use them. The "regulars" at a public house have adopted a ward. Local people without young children of their own befriend young patients, visit them regularly and take them out. Groups of students have spent some weeks of their vacations at various hospitals, helping in whatever ways the staff suggest and in new activities which they initiate. There is almost unlimited scope for more help from more people.

Voluntary help organisers

296. The employment by hospitals of paid voluntary help organisers, usually full-time, is an important new development. Working alongside the voluntary organisations, their aim is to ensure that the contributions of the organisations and of individual volunteers are used to the best advantage. Such appointments have generally been very successful in helping to increase the numbers of volunteers and extend the range of their activities. As with most new developments there have been occasional difficulties; and not unnaturally there have been some doubts among those voluntary organisations already active in the field. This has shown how important it is that the right sort of person should be chosen. Advice is being issued to hospital authorities about the selection of people for this work and the qualities to be looked for.

Voluntary service in the community

Help for families and foster-parents

297. Families with a mentally handicapped member living at home need special help from their neighbours and local voluntary organisations. The effects of a handicapped member on the life of the family are mentioned briefly in Chapter 1. These immediately suggest practical ways in which neighbours can help. The mother of a handicapped child or adult may feel a special need for the friendship of her neighbours and without it be cut off from normal social contact.

298. "Baby-sitting" (whatever the age of the handicapped person) is not only invaluable in giving the parents opportunities for a social life outside the home. It also brings fresh contacts for the handicapped person himself. It is most helpful when organised on a regular basis. Many other forms of help can be given—e.g. with shopping or transport and general good-neighbourliness.

Social activities and recreation

299. The activities mentioned in paragraphs 289 and 290 are just as important for handicapped people living with their families, with foster-parents, in lodgings or in a residential home as they are for those in

hospital.   The brothers and sisters of a severely mentally handicapped child are often deprived of a normal home life; arrangements which give the rest of the family occasional relief from looking after the handicapped member are extremely valuable.   Outings, activities and holidays for the mentally handicapped therefore serve a double purpose, by enriching the life of the handicapped person and also helping the other members of the family.   Arranging holidays for the brothers and sisters is another useful voluntary service.

300.   It may add to the interest of the occasion if a group of handicapped people taken on an outing can include some who do not normally live together—e.g. a group including some from hospital, some from a residential home and some from private homes.   There is scope for infinite variety. It is equally useful to arrange social activities for groups of handicapped people who do already know each other, e.g. through attending a training centre.

301.   Help is needed particularly during school holidays when otherwise the mother may be tied at home and unable to go out even for such things as a visit to the hairdresser.

302.   The adult training centre may provide a focal point for social and recreational activity.   Volunteers can work with the staff, contributing from their personal skills or interests—photography or canoeing, for example.

303.   It is not right to think only in terms of activities specially for the mentally handicapped.   Many can take their place in groups who are not all handicapped—for visits to cinemas, theatres and sports, or in play-groups, youth clubs and old people's clubs.

Help for residential homes
304.   Residents and staff in local authorities' residential homes may need much the same sort of voluntary service as has been mentioned for hospitals —e.g. help in organising hobbies, personal friends for residents not in touch with their own families, funds for extra amenities.

Needs of adults
305.   Voluntary services should not overlook the needs of adults. Children often get the most attention from voluntary sources.   Mentally handicapped adults need it just as much, and there are many more of them.

Voluntary help and the local authorities
306.   Just as hospitals may usefully appoint voluntary help organisers, so also local authorities' social service departments may need to give a lead in identifying needs and suggesting to volunteers how their particular interests and skills can be most effective.   There is also scope for liaison with the hospitals to make the most constructive use of all local resources. Joint arrangements for voluntary service co-ordinators for hospital and local authorities together should be considered.   But public authorities know that they should avoid over-organising.   The essence of voluntary service is that it is freely given, according to the talents and feelings of those who give it.

CHAPTER 8

RESEARCH

Research findings

307. Present attitudes towards the mentally handicapped and views on the services they require are to a significant degree the direct result of research work in recent years. This includes research into the nature and causes of mental handicap; the development of techniques for detecting and correcting secondary handicaps; and studies which have demonstrated mentally handicapped people's considerable capacities for development and the effects of alternative methods of care.

Prevention and detection

308. The present, still limited, techniques of prevention and early detection of mental handicap are described in Chapter 5 and the Appendix. Many of these have been made possible by recent research into chromosomal aberrations, innate metabolic errors, and effects on the fetus of infectious diseases. Several kinds of abnormality in chromosomes have been found to be linked regularly with mental handicap.

309. Techniques have been developed for preventing the progression of physical deformities in mentally handicapped children who in the past would have been confined to a cot or chair. Contractures can be prevented by early surgical treatment, by physiotherapy and by occupational therapy.

310. Better understanding of child development, and techniques of developmental screening, have made it possible to identify deviant development much earlier and take corrective measures.

311. Advances have been made recently in techniques for the detection of visual and auditory defects in people with mental handicap, even the most severely handicapped.

Application of educational techniques

312. Educational techniques have been successfully used, even with very severely mentally handicapped children, to develop verbal and social skills including self-care in such things as washing, dressing and feeding. These techniques include operant conditioning and discrimination learning.

Effect of social environment

313. It has been demonstrated that an appropriately stimulating environment leads to positive improvement in the abilities of mentally handicapped children. Children living with their own families have been shown to be much less backward in social development than children of similar intelligence in institutional care. Within hospitals children cared for in small groups improved significantly in speech and social behaviour compared with those who remained in large wards. Even where children are living at home, attendance at a nursery school or class has been shown to help to provide environmental stimulation.

314. Studies of children and adolescents have demonstrated that those who come from poor and intellectually impoverished homes show a marked improvement in their assessed intelligence when placed in a more stimulating environment.

Studies of residential homes

315. A research study of local authority residential homes in one county has given some indication of the possibilities and limitations of rehabilitation of institutionalised mentally handicapped patients. It was hoped that these homes would be used for short-stay rehabilitation of patients discharged from hospital, to be followed by return to a more independent life. This has proved possible only in a few cases, and some of the more severely handicapped have had to return to hospital. Those who have been able to move from the homes to a less supervised environment (mainly their own family home) seem to have achieved a stable adjustment, but the majority have been shown to require long-term residential care. This together with successful admissions to the homes direct from the family has demonstrated the need for more local authority residential homes.

Value of research findings

316. All this has given us new knowledge of great value. If put to good use, in this country and abroad, it will have a very substantial effect on future generations, by some (still very limited) prevention of mental handicap and considerable reduction of the severity of its effects. But there are still many important gaps in our knowledge, which we may hope will be filled through further research.

Scope for further research

317. There are many branches of knowledge which are relevant to the problems of mental handicap. These include many medical specialities, psychology, sociology and education. Researches in any or all of these fields may be helpful.

318. Particular areas in which knowledge is far from complete include: the causes of many types of mental handicap; the genetic and metabolic factors already recognised as causes; early detection of severe handicapping conditions; the effects of severe psychiatric disorder in childhood; methods of detecting the less severe forms of mental handicap; teaching and work-training; techniques for modifying behaviour problems in mentally handicapped adults; statistical information about the present numbers of mentally handicapped people and their characteristics, and the evaluation of such information; the effect of social environment; the effects of different methods of providing hospital services.

319. It will be important to evaluate the services described in Chapter 5 as they develop, particularly those still at an early stage of development such as parent counselling, and the new patterns of hospital services mentioned in Chapters 5 and 6.

Research in progress

320. Research at present being carried out under the auspices of, or supported by, the Medical Research Council or the Department of Health and Social Security includes:

Genetic and metabolic aspects of mental handicap

    (i) Work in the Medical Research Council's units for metabolic studies, clinical genetics, neuropsychiatry and brain metabolism.

    (ii) Research supported by the Medical Research Council at two hospitals for the mentally handicapped on genetic and metabolic aspects of mental handicap.

    (iii) Diagnostic amniocentesis and clinical cytogenetic work at a paediatric research unit in a teaching hospital.

Psychiatric case registers and other epidemiological studies

    (iv) The compilation of psychiatric case registers in Salford, Camberwell and the Wessex hospital region, which are already providing detailed information on the use of services for the mentally handicapped and material for the evaluation of these services.

    (v) A study of mentally handicapped people in Newcastle for similar purposes.

Abnormalities in development

    (vi) A study of the possible relationship between pre-natal nutrition and abnormalities in the development of fetuses and infants.

    (vii) A comparative study of methods of detecting delayed and aberrant development.

    (viii) A comparative study of the development of children with Down's syndrome (mongolism), who have attended "special care clinics" or play groups before school age and whose parents have received regular counselling, and of children from families who have not received such services.

Special problems of mentally handicapped children

    (ix) Research on the dental problems of physically and mentally handicapped children.

    (x) Evaluation of work in a hospital unit for blind mentally handicapped children.

The implications of mental handicap for families

    (xi) A programme of research into the upbringing of handicapped (including mentally handicapped) and deprived children.

    (xii) Studies of children with special needs (including mentally handicapped children in relation to their families and to society) and of relevant services.

    (xiii) A study of families with a mentally handicapped member compared with a control group of families without such handicap, to examine the problems experienced by the family, and the social factors which may lead to the admission of the handicapped member to hospital.

The development of special educational and treatment methods

(xiv) A study of the learning processes of the mentally handicapped. (The Department of Education and Science will join the Department of Health and Social Security in supporting this from 1972.)

(xv) The development of language teaching methods for mentally retarded children.

(xvi) A study of the application of operant training techniques in the treatment of severely mentally handicapped children.

Evaluation of services

(xvii) An evaluation of residential care for the mentally handicapped in Wessex.

(xviii) A feasibility study for the development and evaluation of modern community-based services for the mentally handicapped in Sheffield County Borough.

(xix) Evaluation of local residential care and the effect of hostel placement in Lancashire.

(xx) Studies of the functions of a regional and district assessment centre for children with multiple handicaps.

APPENDIX

PREVENTION AND EARLY DETECTION

1. The advances in scientific knowledge and in methods of detection, which now make prevention of mental handicap possible in certain limited circumstances, are mostly quite recent.

2. Genetic counselling aims to explain to parents the risk of transmitting certain types of hereditary diseases; where there seems high risk of the birth of a handicapped child, parents can then seek help from the family planning service to prevent conception. At present such counselling is only possible where one affected child is already born. Developments in carrier detection may make it possible in the future to identify some parents at risk before they have had an affected child. Research is continuing into the detection of chromosomal and biochemical abnormalities early in the ante-natal period together with the offer of termination of pregnancy in appropriate cases.

3. The association between rubella infection in a pregnant woman and abnormalities, including occasionally mental handicap, in the fetus is well known. The recent development of a rubella vaccine now gives hope of prevention.

4. One of the most encouraging advances in recent years has been the discovery of a way, by the use of anti-D-immunoglobulin, to prevent haemolytic disease of the newborn, a condition arising from rhesus factor incompatability between the blood of the mother and her child which can cause mental handicap.

5. Detailed surveillance throughout the ante-natal period, in the interests of the child, has assumed greater importance, as more accurate methods are perfected for monitoring fetal growth and development. This requires co-operation between obstetricians and paediatricians, with the object of preventing or reducing the incidence of low-weight births which carry risk of handicap.

6. Expert care during labour enables birth asphyxia to be detected at an early stage and treated so as to prevent damage to the infant's brain.

7. Recent studies suggest that modern intensive care during the neo-natal period of low birth weight babies and others can prevent mental and physical handicap.

8. Since 1964 there have been arrangements for the notification of congenital malformations, including Down's syndrome (frequently called mongolism), which are apparent at birth. Local health authorities keep under special review the care and progress of children notified under these arrangements.

9. Screening of all newborn infants for phenylketonuria, introduced within the last 10 years, is now well established. This allows the small number of children in whom this condition is detected to be given the special diet which may prevent or reduce the severe mental handicap which would otherwise result.

10. It is possible to detect some other defects in a young child and to give early treatment and training which modifies the severity of the eventual handicap. This requires a full medical examination, including a neurological examination, of every infant in the early weeks of life. Such examinations are limited in practice by shortage of paediatricians or other specially trained doctors, and in this situation they are concentrated on children known to be at risk.

11. The report on Child Welfare Centres published in 1967 recommended that local health authorities should maintain registers of children at risk of developing handicapping conditions, for example where adverse factors occurred in the family history, during a mother's pregnancy or at the child's birth. The child's progress is then given special attention by the family doctor and the local authority's child health services, with a view to detecting any handicap at the earliest possible stage.

12. Developmental screening by observation of slow or deviant development is being increasingly practised in child health clinics and by family doctors throughout the country.

13. These developments represent a notable but still very limited advance in means of prevention and early detection. But they are all comparatively recent and not yet fully operating. Moreover, early detection is of little use unless followed by adequate diagnosis and assessment, and by appropriate services for each handicapped child and its family.

Produced in England for Her Majesty's Stationery Office by Commercial Colour Press London

Dd.294205 K20 11/76 CCP